وَلَقَدْ يَسَّرْنَا الْقُرْآنَ لِلذِّكْرِ
فَهَلْ مِن مُّدَّكِرٍ

And We have certainly made the Qur'an easy to *Remember.*
So is there anyone who will be *Reminded.*

(Surah Al-Qamar (54:17))

القرآن الكريم

Surah 77-114

QURANIC
Blueprint

Part 3

From Revelation to Reflection:
Your Guide to Every Surah's Message

Compiled by:
Mufti Kamil Sheikh (MEd)

Empowered Publications®

Living by the Quran: Transforming Knowledge into Action

The Quran is not merely a book to be recited—it is a divine guide meant to shape every aspect of our lives. It provides wisdom for our spiritual growth, ethical conduct, social interactions, and personal development. By internalizing its teachings and applying them in daily life, we move beyond knowledge to action, embodying the principles that lead to success in this world and the Hereafter.

THE QURAN AS A COMPLETE GUIDE FOR LIFE

The Quran addresses every dimension of human existence:

- **Spiritual Guidance:** Strengthening our connection with Allah through prayer, remembrance, and sincerity in worship.
- **Ethical Conduct:** Encouraging honesty, patience, gratitude, and humility in all our dealings.
- **Social Responsibility:** Promoting justice, kindness, and respect in our families, communities, and societies.
- **Personal Development:** Teaching self-discipline, emotional resilience, and a purpose-driven life.

By reflecting on the Quran and integrating its principles, we cultivate a mindset that aligns with divine wisdom.

INTERNALIZING QURANIC TEACHINGS

Applying the Quran in daily life requires conscious effort and practical steps, such as:

Decision-Making Based on Quranic Guidance:

- Seeking answers from the Quran when faced with dilemmas.
- Evaluating choices through the lens of justice, sincerity, and morality.
- Trusting in Allah's wisdom while striving to make ethical decisions.

Building Strong Relationships:

- Treating family, friends, and neighbours with kindness and respect.
- Resolving conflicts with patience and fairness.
- Upholding honesty and integrity in all interactions.

Developing Strong Character:

- Practicing humility, gratitude, and self-discipline.
- Controlling anger and responding with wisdom.
- Seeking forgiveness and being forgiving towards others.

PRACTICAL WAYS TO IMPLEMENT QURANIC WISDOM

To truly **live by the Quran**, we can:

- **Reflect (Tadabbur):** Read and ponder over its verses to extract personal lessons.
- **Act (Tafsir in Action):** Implement its teachings in our daily behaviour and choices.
- **Engage (Community Application):** Share its wisdom with others through kindness, service, and good character.

The Quran is meant to **transform hearts, minds, and societies**. When we embrace its teachings with sincerity and effort, we bring its light into our lives—fulfilling its purpose as a guide to truth, righteousness, and ultimate success.

اللَّهُمَّ إِنِّي عَبْدُكَ، ابْنُ عَبْدِكَ، ابْنُ أَمَتِكَ، نَاصِيَتِي بِيَدِكَ، مَاضٍ فِي حُكْمُكَ، عَدْلٌ فِي قَضَاؤُكَ، أَسْأَلُكَ بِكُلِّ
اسْمٍ هُوَ لَكَ سَمَّيْتَ بِهِ نَفْسَكَ، أَوْ أَنْزَلْتَهُ فِي كِتَابِكَ، أَوْ عَلَّمْتَهُ أَحَدًا مِنْ خَلْقِكَ، أَوِ اسْتَأْثَرْتَ بِهِ فِي عِلْمِ
الْغَيْبِ عِنْدَكَ، أَنْ تَجْعَلَ الْقُرْآنَ رَبِيعَ قَلْبِي، وَنُورَ صَدْرِي، وَجَلَاءَ حُزْنِي، وَذَهَابَ هَمِّي

"O Allah, I am Your slave. I am the child of Your male slave and the child of Your female slave, my forelock is in Your hand, Your judgment upon me is assured, Your decree concerning me is just. I ask You by every single name that You have named Yourself with, or that You have revealed in Your book, or taught to one of Your creation, or have completely kept in Your knowledge in the unseen, to make the Qur'an the spring of my heart, and the light of my chest, and let it be the banisher of my sadness and let it be the reliever of my anxiety." (Musnad Ahmed) *Ameen*

CONTENTS

SURAH'S 77 - 114

Revealed in	Juz	Surah No.	No. of verses
Makkah	29	77	50

سُورَةُ الْمُرْسَلَاتِ

SURAH AL-MURSALAT

(THE SENT FORTH)

أَلَمْ نَجْعَلِ ٱلْأَرْضَ كِفَاتًا ۝ أَحْيَآءً وَأَمْوَٰتًا ۝ وَجَعَلْنَا فِيهَا رَوَٰسِىَ شَٰمِخَٰتٍ
وَأَسْقَيْنَٰكُم مَّآءً فُرَاتًا ۝

"Have We not made the earth a lodging for the living and the dead, and placed upon it towering, firm mountains, and given you fresh water to drink?" (77:25-27)

Context

The Surah addresses the disbelievers who denied the Day of Judgment. It aims to reaffirm the reality of the resurrection and the consequences for the rejecters of truth, highlighting that the Day of Reckoning is inevitable. The Surah also reminds people of the signs of Allah's power and authority over creation.

Topics

- The Power & Role of the Angelic Emissaries
- The Certainty of the Day of Judgment
- Destruction of Disbelievers & Reward for Believers
- Allah's Signs in Creation

Theme

The primary theme of Surah Al-Mursalat is the certainty of the Day of Resurrection and the consequences of disbelief. The Surah emphasizes the power of Allah and the inevitability of the events leading to the Day of Judgment. It urges people to heed the warnings given to them and to believe in the divine truth.

Virtues & Benefits

Surah Al-Mursalat emphasizes the importance of believing in the unseen, particularly the Day of Judgment, and acknowledging Allah's absolute power.

Ayah 1-7

The Sworn Angels

In these opening verses, Allah swears by the winds and angels that are dispatched in succession, stirring the air and spreading Allah's message to the world. The angels' tasks include both excusing and warning humanity. The verses assert the certainty of the promised event, which is the Day of Judgment. These oaths highlight the inevitability and importance of the resurrection, urging the listeners to take heed and be prepared for what is to come.

Ayah 8-15

The Day of Decision

The surah continues by describing the catastrophic events that will occur before the Day of Judgment. The stars will vanish, the sky will crack, and the mountains will be scattered. The messengers, who were sent to guide humanity, will be summoned, and the Day of Decision will finally arrive. The verses emphasize the severity of that day and the fate of those who denied the truth, warning them with woe for their lies. The reference to the Day of Decision calls attention to the final and irreversible judgment that awaits.

Ayah 16-22

Reflection on Creation

In these verses, Allah reminds humanity of the fate of those who came before, emphasizing that the ancients were destroyed and replaced with others. This serves as a warning to the rejecters of the truth. The verses also reflect on the humble beginnings of human creation—formed from a small fluid and placed securely in the womb for a predetermined time. This is a reminder of Allah's power in both creation and destruction, urging people to reflect on their mortality and the consequences of rejecting His guidance.

Ayah 23-30

Consequences of Denial & Rejection

These verses highlight Allah's power and the blessings He has bestowed upon humanity, such as the earth as a homestead, mountains for stability, and pure water to drink. Despite these blessings, some continue to deny His signs. The verses forewarn that those who deny the truth will be directed to the punishment they used to reject. The reference to the shadow of three masses symbolizes the overwhelming and inescapable nature of the punishment awaiting them. This serves as a stern reminder of the consequences of disbelief.

Ayah 31-40

The Day of Separation

These verses vividly describe the severity of the punishment on the Day of Judgment. The flames are depicted as shooting sparks like castles or yellow camels, highlighting their intensity. On this day, the liars will be silenced and unable to offer excuses or apologies. The Day of Separation will witness the gathering of all—both the ancient peoples and those present. The rejection of truth will lead to eternal consequences, and there will be no escape for those who falsify or deny the divine message.

Ayah 41-50

Fate of the Righteous & Rejecters

The righteous will find themselves in bliss, enjoying shade, fountains, and fruits, rewarded for their good deeds. They are invited to eat and drink joyfully, a reflection of the kindness they showed in their lives. In stark contrast, the deniers and liars are warned, as they face their consequences. When commanded to humble themselves, they refuse, showing their arrogance and rejection. Their stubbornness leads to eternal loss, and the question arises: what message, beyond the truth they've rejected, will they now accept?

Lessons to Learn

The Day of Judgment is certain, and everyone will be accountable for their actions.

The power of Allah is all-encompassing, and He controls all aspects of creation.

It is important to heed the warnings of the Quran and follow the righteous path to avoid the torment of the Day of Judgment.

Action Steps

Reflect on the signs of Allah in nature and creation, using them to strengthen your belief.

Remind yourself daily of the certainty of the Day of Resurrection and the consequences of actions.

Engage in good deeds, be conscious of your responsibilities, and seek Allah's forgiveness for shortcomings.

Revealed in	Juz	Surah No.	No. of verses
Makkah	30	78	40

سُورَةُ النَّبَإِ

SURAH AN-NABA

(THE GREAT NEWS)

إِنَّآ أَنذَرْنَٰكُمْ عَذَابًا قَرِيبًا يَوْمَ يَنظُرُ ٱلْمَرْءُ مَا قَدَّمَتْ يَدَاهُ وَيَقُولُ ٱلْكَافِرُ يَٰلَيْتَنِى
كُنتُ تُرَٰبًۢا ۝

"Indeed, We have warned you of an imminent punishment—the Day every person will see 'the consequences of' what their hands have done, and the disbelievers will cry, "I wish I were dust." (78:40)

Context

The surah was revealed in response to the disbelief and arguments of the Quraysh regarding the resurrection and the Hereafter. They questioned the concept of life after death mockingly, and this surah provides a clear affirmation of the reality of resurrection, divine justice, and the ultimate consequences of belief and disbelief.

Topics

- The Disbelief of People in Resurrection
- Signs of Allah's creation as Proof of His power
- The Coming of the Day of Judgment
- The Fate of Righteous & Wicked
- The Severity of Hellfire & Bliss of Paradise

Theme

Surah An-Naba focuses on the inevitability of resurrection, divine judgment, and the fate of both the righteous and the wicked. It highlights signs of Allah's creation as evidence of His power and reminds people of the ultimate reality of the Hereafter, where rewards and punishments will be justly distributed.

Virtues & Benefits

Emphasizes the concept of divine justice
Reciting this surah regularly strengthens faith in the afterlife and Allah's ultimate power

Ayah 1-5

The Great News

The surah opens with a rhetorical question about the "Great Event"—the Day of Judgment—which people argue about. The repetition of "Surely, they will find out" intensifies the warning that the reality will soon be clear to all.

Ayah 6-16

Signs of Divine Power

Allah reminds humanity of His signs in creation, such as making the earth a stable cradle, anchoring the mountains as pegs, creating humans in pairs, providing sleep as a source of rest, alternating night and day, raising the heavens with strength, illuminating the world with the sun as a blazing lamp, and sending rain to bring life to the earth. These signs affirm that if Allah has created such a perfect world, He is surely capable of resurrecting humanity for judgment.

Ayah 17-30

The Day of Sorting

The "Day of Sorting" will begin with the Trumpet being blown. The heavens will open like gateways, and mountains will vanish. Hell will be waiting as an ambush for the wicked, where they will neither find comfort nor relief, only boiling water and freezing hail as punishment. This suffering is a direct result of their denial and lack of accountability.

Ayah 31-36

Triumph of the Righteous

In contrast, the righteous will enter gardens with vineyards, pure companions, and refreshing drinks. The atmosphere will be one of peace—free from gossip and lies. This is described as a "fitting gift" from the Merciful Lord.

Ayah 37-40

The Final Warning

The chapter ends with a solemn reminder: on that Day, none will speak except by Allah's permission. The reality of judgment is inevitable, and people are urged to turn back to their Lord. The regret of the disbelievers will be so intense that they will wish to be reduced to dust rather than face the consequences of their actions. This surah powerfully emphasizes both the justice and mercy of Allah, urging reflection before the ultimate reality arrives.

Ayah 1-40

Summary of Surah Naba

Surah An-Naba (78) discusses the Day of Judgment and the contrast between believers and disbelievers. It opens with a rhetorical question about the great news (the resurrection) that people dispute. The surah highlights Allah's signs in creation, like the earth, mountains, and the cycle of day and night, as proof of His power. It then describes the horrors of the Day of Resurrection, the fate of disbelievers in Hell, and the rewards of Paradise for the righteous. The surah concludes by affirming the certainty of divine justice and warning of the impending reality of the Hereafter.

Lessons to Learn

The resurrection is real and inevitable
Everything in creation points to Allah's power and wisdom
Belief and righteous actions lead to eternal rewards
Disbelief and arrogance result in severe consequences
Life is temporary, and we should prepare for the Hereafter

Action Steps

Strive to live righteously, knowing that all actions have consequences
Avoid arrogance and heed the warnings about Hellfire
Seek Allah's guidance and mercy through regular prayer and repentance

Revealed in	Juz	Surah No.	No. of verses
Makkah	30	79	46

سُورَةُ النَّازِعَاتِ

SURAH AN-NAZIYAT

(THE SNATCHERS)

وَأَمَّا مَنْ خَافَ مَقَامَ رَبِّهِ وَنَهَى ٱلنَّفْسَ عَنِ ٱلْهَوَىٰ ۝ فَإِنَّ ٱلْجَنَّةَ هِىَ ٱلْمَأْوَىٰ ۝

"And as for those who were in awe of standing before their Lord and restrained themselves from 'evil' desires, Paradise will certainly be 'their' home." (79:40-41)

Context

This Surah was revealed in response to the Quraysh's doubts about the Resurrection. The people of Makkah rejected the idea of life after death, questioning how the dead could be raised. Allah responds by describing the power of the angels, the fate of past nations, and the certainty of the Hereafter. The example of Pharaoh is given to show the consequences of arrogance and disbelief.

Topics

- The Oath by Angels
- Scenes of the Day of Judgment
- The Power & Control of Allah
- The Pharaoh's Arrogance & Destruction
- The Fate of Righteous & Wicked
- The Inevitability of the Hereafter

Theme

The Surah revolves around death, resurrection, and accountability. It begins with oaths about the angels who manage the souls of the dead, followed by scenes of the Day of Judgment. It contrasts the fate of the rebellious with that of the righteous. The arrogance of Pharaoh serves as a warning, and the Surah ends by affirming that the Hereafter is near, even if people doubt it.

Virtues & Benefits

Reflecting on Pharaoh's arrogance helps strengthen humility and obedience to Allah.
It teaches reliance on Allah's justice; wrongdoers will be punished, & the righteous will be rewarded.

Ayah 1-5

The Oath of the Angels

The chapter begins with a series of oaths by different types of angels—those who seize souls violently, those who remove them gently, those who glide smoothly through the heavens, those who race ahead to execute divine commands, and those who regulate the affairs of the universe. These oaths highlight the power and precision with which divine decrees unfold.

Ayah 6-14

Terror of the Resurrection

The surah describes the great cosmic quake, followed by another upheaval, which will leave hearts pounding and eyes downcast in terror. The disbelievers, who doubted resurrection, will realize that it happens in an instant, like a single call that brings them back to life.

Ayah 15-26

The Story of Pharaoh's Arrogance

The narrative of Prophet Musa (AS) and Pharaoh serves as a warning against arrogance and defiance. Despite witnessing miracles, Pharaoh arrogantly proclaimed himself "the most high." Consequently, Allah seized him with an exemplary punishment, showing that power and tyranny cannot stand against divine justice.

Ayah 27-33

The Signs of Divine Creation

Allah calls humanity to reflect on the creation of the universe—the vast sky, the structured cosmos, the alternating night and day, the spread-out earth, and the provision of water, vegetation, and mountains. These signs serve as evidence of God's ability to resurrect and hold humanity accountable.

Ayah 34-41

Fate of Defiant & Righteous

When the Great Cataclysm arrives, every soul will be confronted with its deeds. Those who were defiant and prioritized worldly desires over faith will find Hell as their abode. In contrast, those who feared their Lord and restrained their desires will enter Paradise.

Ayah 42-46

The Mystery of the Hour

The disbelievers persistently ask about the exact timing of the Hour. However, the Prophet ﷺ is reminded that its knowledge belongs solely to Allah. His role is to warn those who are willing to heed. When the Hour finally comes, it will feel as if life was merely a fleeting moment.

Lessons to Learn

The power of Allah over life, death, and resurrection is absolute.

The Hereafter is real and inevitable.

Arrogance and denial, like Pharaoh's, lead to destruction.

The world is temporary; real success lies in fearing Allah and preparing for the next life.

Action Steps

Reflect on the certainty of death and prepare for the Hereafter.

Avoid arrogance and always remain humble before Allah.

Strengthen faith in resurrection by contemplating Allah's creation.

Be mindful of the Day of Judgment in daily actions.

سُورَةُ عَبَسَ

Revealed in	Juz	Surah No.	No. of verses
Makkah	30	80	42

SURAH ABASA

(HE FROWNED)

فَإِذَا جَآءَتِ ٱلصَّآخَّةُ ۝ يَوْمَ يَفِرُّ ٱلْمَرْءُ مِنْ أَخِيهِ ۝ وَأُمِّهِۦ وَأَبِيهِ ۝ وَصَـٰحِبَتِهِۦ وَبَنِيهِ ۝

"Then, when the Deafening Blast comes to pass— on that Day every person will flee from their own siblings, and 'even' their mother and father, and 'even' their spouse and children." (80:33-36)

Context

This Surah was revealed when Abdullah ibn Umm Maktum, a blind companion, came to Prophet Muhammad ﷺ seeking guidance while he was engaged in a discussion with Quraysh leaders. The Prophet ﷺ frowned and turned away, prioritising the elite over the blind man. Allah revealed this Surah to remind that divine guidance is for all and should not favour the powerful over the sincere.

Topics

- Incident of Prophet ﷺ & blind man
- Importance of Divine Revelation
- Allah's Blessings & Provisions for Humanity
- Horrors of the Day of Judgement

Theme

The Surah emphasises equality in seeking knowledge and Allah's concern for all human beings, regardless of status. It reminds that arrogance and worldly rank do not determine one's worth in the sight of Allah. The Surah also describes the Quran as a divine reminder, discusses the blessings of creation, and warns of the consequences of ignoring Allah's message.

Virtues & Benefits

It teaches humility and inclusivity in da'wah.It highlights the importance of the Quran as a divine reminder.It warns against arrogance and prioritising worldly status.

Ayah 1-10
The Lesson in Priorities

The chapter begins with an incident where the Prophet Muhammad ﷺ momentarily turned away from a blind man who sincerely sought guidance, giving preference to influential people instead. This serves as a reminder that true worth is based on sincerity and piety, not social status. The Quran highlights that those who seek purification and sincere remembrance should be prioritised over those who are indifferent.

Ayah 11-16
Divine Message & Its Preservation

The Quran is described as a sacred revelation, preserved in honored pages, recorded by noble and devoted scribes. This emphasizes the purity and authenticity of the message, ensuring that it remains unchanged and accessible to those who seek guidance.

Ayah 17-23
The Thanklessness of Man

Man is reminded of his humble origin—from a mere drop of fluid—yet he often remains ungrateful to his Creator. Allah facilitated his journey in life, from birth to death, and will resurrect him when He wills. Despite these blessings, man fails to fulfill the divine commands.

Ayah 24-32
Reflection on Divine Provisions

Allah directs mankind to reflect on the blessings of nature: the rain that nourishes the earth, the crops, fruits, and lush gardens provided for sustenance. These are signs of Allah's mercy and power, yet many take them for granted.

Ayah 33-42
The Day of Judgement

The chapter concludes with a vivid description of the Day of Judgment. The Deafening Noise (the great blast) will cause people to abandon even their closest relationships, consumed by their own fate. Some faces will shine with joy and laughter, having attained salvation, while others will be covered in sorrow and regret—those who denied the truth and acted wickedly.

Ayah 1-42
Conclusion of Surah

Surah Abasa serves as a profound reminder of humility, sincerity, and the true priorities in life. It teaches that guidance and faith are not reserved for the elite but are accessible to all who seek them, regardless of status. The Surah emphasises gratitude for Allah's blessings, the certainty of resurrection, and the consequences of one's choices on the Day of Judgement. It urges reflection on divine provisions and warns of the stark contrast between those who attain salvation and those who face regret in the Hereafter.

Lessons to Learn

Prioritize sincerity over social status – everyone deserves guidance.

The Quran is a noble and sacred message, meant for all humanity.

Reflect on the blessings of creation and be grateful.

Remember the reality of the Hereafter and prepare for it.

Action Steps

Show kindness to everyone, regardless of their social status.

Dedicate time to understanding the Quran as it is the ultimate guidance.

Be grateful for the blessings of food, shelter, and provisions.

Reflect on death and the Hereafter to keep life in perspective.

Revealed in	Juz	Surah No.	No. of verses
Makkah	30	81	29

سُورَةُ التَّكْوِيرِ

SURAH AT-TAKWIR

(THE DARKENING)

فَأَيْنَ تَذْهَبُونَ ۝ إِنْ هُوَ إِلَّا ذِكْرٌ لِّلْعَٰلَمِينَ ۝ لِمَن شَآءَ مِنكُمْ أَن يَسْتَقِيمَ ۝

"So what 'other' path would you take? Surely this 'Quran' is only a reminder to the whole world— to whoever of you wills to take the Straight Way." (81:26-28)

Context

This Surah was revealed in the early Makkan period when the Prophet ﷺ was calling people to Islam. It describes the horrifying events of the Last Day and the truthfulness of the Qur'an and Prophet Muhammad ﷺ. The Surah refutes the doubts of the disbelievers and affirms that the Quran is a divine revelation brought by Angel Jibreel (AS).

Topics

- Destruction on Judgement Day
- Accountability for actions
- Questioning of buried girls
- Quran's authenticity & Jibril's (AS) role
- Disbelievers' response to truth

Theme

Surah At-Takwir emphasises the inevitability of the Day of Judgement by describing cosmic destruction. It highlights the certainty of divine revelation & warns against rejecting faith. The Surah presents powerful imagery of the sun darkening, stars falling, mountains vanishing, & the resurrection of souls. The Quran is confirmed as the truth conveyed by a trustworthy Angel Jibril (AS).

Virtues & Benefits

Prophet Muhammad ﷺ said: "Whoever wants to see the Day of Judgment as if they are seeing it with their own eyes, let them recite Surah At-Takwir, Al-Infitar, and Al-Inshiqaq." (Tirmidhi)

Ayah 1-13

Signs of the Final Hour

The chapter begins with a powerful depiction of the events leading up to the Day of Judgment. The sun will lose its light, the stars will fade, and the mountains will move from their places. Relationships between people will be severed, wild beasts will be gathered together, and the oceans will be set on fire. Souls will be reunited with their bodies, and the innocent victims of injustice—such as the girl buried alive—will be questioned, emphasizing ultimate divine justice.

Ayah 14

Moment of Awareness

On that Day, every soul will realize the consequences of its deeds. The records of actions will be exposed, revealing every detail of a person's life. Paradise will be brought near for the righteous, while Hellfire will be ignited for the wicked.

Ayah 15-18

The Truth of Revelation

Allah swears by the galaxies in their precise orbits, the retreating night, and the fresh breath of morning. These oaths highlight the order and power in the universe, reinforcing the truth of the message that follows.

Ayah 19-25

Messenger and His Authenticity

The Quran then shifts to affirm the credibility of the Prophet Muhammad ﷺ. It describes the Quran as the words of a noble and powerful messenger, referring to Angel Jibreel (Gabriel), who is honoured in the presence of Allah. The Prophet ﷺ is neither possessed nor deceived; rather, he witnessed the angel on the luminous horizon. Unlike false prophets or devils, he does not withhold knowledge of the unseen.

Ayah 26-29

The Call to Guidance

The chapter concludes with a direct question: Where are you heading? The Quran is a reminder for all of humanity, but guidance is only for those who choose to follow the straight path. However, ultimate will and guidance rest with Allah alone, reminding us of His absolute authority over all things.

Ayah 1-29

Conclusion of Surah

Surah At-Takwir presents a vivid portrayal of the upheaval on the Day of Judgement, emphasising the collapse of the natural order and the accountability of every soul. It highlights the truthfulness of the Quran and the authenticity of its messenger, reinforcing that divine revelation is free from falsehood. The Surah concludes by reminding humanity that guidance is available for those who seek it, but ultimately, Allah's will prevails. It serves as a powerful call to reflect, prepare for the Hereafter, and remain steadfast in faith.

Lessons to Learn

- The world will end, & every soul will be held accountable.
- Injustice will be exposed, and even the weakest will get justice on the Day of Judgement.
- The Quran is a divine truth, and rejecting it leads to destruction.
- Angel Jibril (AS) is an honoured messenger, and the revelation he brought is authentic.

Action Steps

- Strengthen your faith by remembering the Day of Judgement.
- Uphold justice and protect the weak, especially women and children.
- Believe in the authenticity of the Quran and study it deeply.
- Avoid arrogance and heedlessness; reflect on Allah's signs in the universe.

Revealed in	Juz	Surah No.	No. of verses
Makkah	30	82	19

سُورَةُ الانفِطَارِ

SURAH AL-INFITAR

(THE CLEAVING)

يَٰٓأَيُّهَا ٱلْإِنسَٰنُ مَا غَرَّكَ بِرَبِّكَ ٱلْكَرِيمِ ۝

"O humanity! What has emboldened you against your Lord, the Most Generous," (82:6)

Context

Surah Al-Infitar was revealed in the early Makkan period when the disbelievers were rejecting the concept of the Day of Judgement and accountability. This Surah vividly describes the destruction of the cosmos and resurrection of human beings. It emphasises that every action is recorded by angels and that people will be judged based on their deeds.

Topics

- Destruction of the universe
- Resurrection & accountability
- Role of Honorable Recording Angels
- The Division Between the Righteous and the Wicked in the Hereafter.
- The Power and Mercy of Allah.

Theme

Surah Al-Infitar focuses on the catastrophic events of the Last Day, emphasising human accountability before Allah. It serves as a wake-up call for people to recognise that nothing in this world is permanent, and that each person's actions will be recorded and presented on the Day of Judgement. It also highlights Allah's mercy and justice, reminding people to prepare for the Hereafter.

Virtues & Benefits

Prophet Muhammad ﷺ said: "Whoever wants to see the Day of Judgement as if they are seeing it with their own eyes, let them recite Surah At-Takwir, Al-Infitar, and Al-Inshiqaq." (Tirmidhi)

Ayah 1-4

The Cosmic Upheaval

The chapter begins with a vivid description of the end times, when the natural order of the universe will be completely overturned. The sky will break apart, the planets will scatter, the vast oceans will explode, and the graves will be overturned, exposing what was hidden. This imagery signifies the total destruction of the world as we know it, marking the beginning of the afterlife.

Ayah 5

The Moment of Realization

On that Day, every soul will come to know the truth of its actions—both the good it sent forward and the deeds it neglected. No action, however small, will be lost; everything will be revealed in perfect justice.

Ayah 6-8

Rebuke to Human Arrogance

The Quran then directly addresses humanity, questioning why people are deceived about their Lord, despite His generosity and perfection. Allah, in His wisdom, created, shaped, and proportioned every human being in a unique and precise form. Yet, instead of being grateful and obedient, people turn away from the truth.

Ayah 9-12

The Ever-Watchful Recorders

The passage highlights the presence of divine recorders—noble and trustworthy angels who document every human action. These angels do not miss anything, ensuring that complete justice is carried out on the Day of Judgment. This serves as both a reassurance for the righteous and a warning for those who persist in wrongdoing.

Ayah 13-16

Fate of the Righteous & Wicked

A clear contrast is drawn between the two groups: the righteous will enjoy everlasting bliss, while the wicked will face the torment of Hell. The punishment is inescapable, and once they enter, they will not be removed from it.

Ayah 17-19

The Day of Absolute Justice

The chapter closes with an emphatic repetition, reinforcing the severity of the Day of Judgment. On that Day, no soul will be able to help another, and ultimate authority will belong to Allah alone. This final reminder emphasizes the importance of accountability and submission to divine truth.

Lessons to Learn

- The world will be destroyed, and everything is temporary.
- Every action is recorded, and no deed—good or bad—goes unnoticed.
- Allah is the Most Merciful, but also the Most Just.
- Human beings are deceived by worldly distractions and must wake up before it is too late.

Action Steps

- Strengthen belief in the Hereafter and live with accountability.
- Remember that Allah created you perfectly and express gratitude.
- Be mindful of your actions since angels record everything.
- Repent sincerely and seek Allah's forgiveness before it's too late.

Revealed in	Juz	Surah No.	No. of verses
Makkah	30	83	36

سُورَةُ المُطَفِّفِين

SURAH AL-MUTAFFIFIN

(THE DEFRAUDERS)

وَيْلٌ لِّلْمُطَفِّفِينَ ۝

"Woe to the defrauders!" (83:1)

Context

This Surah was revealed to condemn corrupt business practices, particularly dishonest merchants who cheat in measuring and weighing goods. The Quraysh and other traders in Mecca were known to exploit buyers while demanding full measure for themselves. The Surah warns about the Day of Judgement, where the righteous will be rewarded and the wicked, especially those who deceive others, will face severe punishment.

Topics

- Condemnation of Dishonest Business Dealings.
- The Certainty of the Day of Judgment.
- The Fate of the Wicked
- The Rewards of the Righteous
- The mockery of the disbelievers and their eventual regret.

Theme

Surah Al-Mutaffifin highlights the importance of honesty in financial transactions and condemns fraud and injustice. It contrasts the fate of the wicked (those who cheat and deny the truth) with the blessed fate of the righteous. It also emphasises the certainty of divine justice and the existence of two records—Sijjin (for the wicked) and Illiyyeen (for the righteous)—which will determine people's destiny in the Hereafter.

Virtues & Benefits

Teaches the importance of honesty and fair dealings in all aspects of life. Encourages belief in the Hereafter. Reveals the concept of divine justice, proving that no action goes unnoticed.

Ayah 1-6

The Warning to the Fraudulent

The chapter opens with a warning to those who cheat in business transactions. These people demand full measure when taking from others but shortchange when giving. This injustice is condemned, as it reflects dishonesty and selfishness. The passage reminds them that they will be resurrected on a great and terrifying Day, standing before Allah, the Lord of all worlds, to answer for their deeds.

Ayah 7-17

The Fate of the Wicked

The record of the wicked is kept in Sijjeen, a register of the condemned. The Quran questions the listener—how can they comprehend the gravity of Sijjeen? It is a precise record of sins, ensuring full accountability. The deniers of the Last Day are warned, especially those who mock the scriptures and dismiss them as "ancient legends." Their denial has corrupted their hearts, covering them with rust due to their sinful choices. On Judgment Day, they will be veiled from their Lord, a devastating punishment, and will be cast into Hell as a consequence of their arrogance.

Ayah 18-28

The Reward of the Righteous

In contrast, the record of the righteous is preserved in Elliyyeen, a register of honor. The Quran again asks—how can one comprehend the grandeur of Elliyyeen? It is a written record, witnessed by those closest to Allah, such as the angels. The righteous will enjoy supreme bliss, seated on magnificent thrones, with their faces radiating joy. They will drink a special sealed wine, whose aroma is like musk, mixed with Tasneem, a pure and exclusive spring for those nearest to Allah. This passage urges people to compete in seeking this divine reward.

Ayah 29-33

The Mockery of the Believers

The chapter recalls how, in the worldly life, the disbelievers mocked and ridiculed the believers. They would laugh at them, wink in scorn, and boast among themselves, seeing the believers as misguided. They returned to their families in arrogance, believing their rejection of faith made them superior. However, they had no authority to judge others, nor were they given control over people's fate.

Ayah 34-36

The Ultimate Justice

On the Day of Judgement, the roles will be reversed. The believers will laugh at the disbelievers as they recline in comfort, watching their former oppressors face the consequences of their mockery. The passage ends with a rhetorical question, emphasising that the disbelievers will be fully repaid for their actions—justice will prevail, and every soul will receive its due.

Ayah 1-36

Conclusion of Surah

Surah Al-Mutaffifin highlights the consequences of dishonesty and arrogance, warning those who cheat and mock faith of their fate in Sijjin, while assuring the righteous of their reward in Illiyyin. It reinforces the certainty of divine justice, where every deed will be accounted for. The Surah serves as a call to uphold honesty, integrity, and faith in Allah's ultimate judgment.

Lessons to Learn

- Honesty and integrity in trade, business, and daily life are crucial.
- Cheating and deception will bring divine punishment.
- Every action is recorded, and we will be judged accordingly.
- The righteous may face ridicule in this world, but their ultimate success is in the Hereafter.

Action Steps

- Be honest in financial transactions, whether selling, buying, or measuring.
- Strengthen faith in the Hereafter by remembering the reward of the righteous and punishment of the wicked.
- Remain patient if ridiculed for righteousness, knowing that Allah's judgement is final.

Revealed in	Juz	Surah No.	No. of verses
Makkah	30	84	25

سُورَةُ الانشِقَاقِ

SURAH AL-INSHIQAQ

(THE SPLITTING)

يَٰٓأَيُّهَا ٱلْإِنسَٰنُ إِنَّكَ كَادِحٌ إِلَىٰ رَبِّكَ كَدْحًا فَمُلَٰقِيهِ

"O humanity! Indeed, you are labouring restlessly towards your Lord, and will 'eventually' meet the consequences." (84:6)

Context

This Surah describes the events of the Last Day when the sky will split apart and the earth will lay bare all that was hidden. It emphasises that human beings are constantly progressing toward their final meeting with Allah. It warns of the two ultimate destinations: Paradise for the righteous and punishment for the deniers. The Surah also highlights how some people will receive their record in their right hand (salvation) while others in their left hand (destruction).

Topics

- Cataclysmic Events of the Last Day
- Every Soul's journey toward Allah
- Fate of the Righteous & Wicked
- Denial of the Hereafter & its Consequences.

Theme

Surah Al-Inshiqaq focuses on the reality of the Afterlife, portraying the inevitable transformation of the universe on the Day of Judgement. It emphasises that every human being is on a journey toward their ultimate reckoning. The righteous will be granted ease and rewards, while the disbelievers will face misery and torment. The Surah concludes with a stern reminder that nothing is hidden from Allah and every action will be accounted for.

Virtues & Benefits

Reminds believers of the certainty of the Day of Judgement. Encourages righteous deeds by highlighting the rewards of Paradise. Warns against arrogance and denial of the Hereafter.

Ayah 1-5

The Cosmic Upheaval

The chapter begins by describing the Day of Judgement, when the sky will be ruptured, obeying the command of its Lord. The earth will be flattened and will cast out everything hidden within it—graves will be emptied, and secrets will be exposed. These verses emphasise that the universe itself submits to Allah's will, setting the stage for the final reckoning.

Ayah 6-9

The Fate of the Righteous

Addressing humanity, the Quran reminds that every person is on a journey toward their Lord, inevitably meeting Him. Those who receive their record in their right hand will have an easy reckoning, symbolising Allah's mercy upon them. They will return to their families in joy, representing their entry into Paradise, where they will reunite with loved ones in eternal bliss.

Ayah 10-15

The Fate of the Wicked

In contrast, those who receive their record behind their back—indicating disgrace—will cry out in despair, wishing for death to escape their fate. They will be cast into the Fire, a consequence of their arrogance and false sense of security in worldly pleasures. They lived in heedlessness, thinking they would never be held accountable, but Allah was always aware of their actions.

Ayah 16-19

The Oath by Natural Phenomena

Allah swears by the twilight, the night, and the full moon—elements that signify change and cycles in creation. These transitions reflect the journey of human life and the inevitable stages one must pass through, ultimately leading to death and resurrection. The phrase "You will mount stage by stage" signifies that human beings are constantly progressing toward their final destination, whether they realise it or not.

Ayah 20-24

The Denial of the Disbelievers

Despite clear signs, many people refuse to believe. Even when the Quran is recited, they do not humble themselves before it. Their rejection is not due to ignorance but stubborn denial. Allah, who knows their inner thoughts, warns them of a painful punishment, reinforcing that disbelief is not just an external rejection but a condition of the heart.

Ayah 25

The Reward of the Believers

The chapter concludes with hope for those who believe and perform righteous deeds. Unlike the punishment of the wicked, their reward will be eternal and undiminished, emphasising Allah's justice and mercy. Faith and good actions lead to an everlasting reward, free from loss or suffering.

Lessons to Learn

- The universe will submit to Allah's command on the Last Day.
- Every human is on a journey toward their final judgement.
- Our deeds determine whether we will receive our book in the right or left hand.
- Life is temporary, and the Hereafter is the true reality.

Action Steps

- Avoid arrogance and heedlessness, as they lead to regret in the Hereafter.
- Acknowledge the signs of Allah in the universe as proof of resurrection.
- Remember that no deed is hidden—everything will be exposed on the Day of Judgement.

Revealed in	Juz	Surah No.	No. of verses
Makkah	30	85	22

سُورَةُ البُرُوجِ

SURAH AL-BUROOJ

(THE GREAT STARS)

إِنَّ ٱلَّذِينَ ءَامَنُوا۟ وَعَمِلُوا۟ ٱلصَّٰلِحَٰتِ لَهُمْ جَنَّٰتٌ تَجْرِى مِن تَحْتِهَا ٱلْأَنْهَٰرُ ذَٰلِكَ ٱلْفَوْزُ ٱلْكَبِيرُ ۝

"Surely those who believe and do good will have Gardens under which rivers flow. That is the greatest triumph." (85:11)

Context

This Surah was revealed to console the Prophet Muhammad ﷺ and his followers during the early persecution in Mecca. It recounts the story of a past nation that tortured believers by burning them in a ditch for their faith. The Surah assures the believers that Allah is aware of their suffering and that the oppressors will face severe consequences. The power of Allah and the certainty of resurrection are also emphasised.

Topics

- Oath by the sky and constellations.
- The story of the persecuted believers burned in the trench.
- The fate of the tyrants and the reward of the righteous.
- Allah's power over the universe.

Theme

Surah Al-Burooj highlights the persecution of believers, the inevitable punishment for the tyrants, and the reward for the steadfast believers. It draws from a historical event where innocent believers were burned alive for their faith, showing that Allah watches over His servants and will hold the oppressors accountable. The Surah reassures that the believers' sacrifices are not in vain, and they will receive eternal rewards in the Hereafter.

Virtues & Benefits

Encourages patience and steadfastness in times of hardship. Reminds believers that oppression will not go unpunished. Assures that faith in Allah leads to ultimate success.

Ayah 1-3
The Oaths by the Sky

Allah swears by the sky adorned with constellations, symbolising His supreme control over the universe. He then calls attention to the Promised Day, the Day of Judgement, reinforcing its certainty. The verse also refers to the witness and the witnessed, which can mean those who testify and those who are testified against, indicating divine justice where every action is accounted for.

Ayah 4-9
Tragedy of the People of the Trench

The People of the Trench were a tyrannical group who persecuted believers by burning them alive in a fire fuelled by their cruelty. They watched, unmoved, as the faithful suffered, demonstrating the extent of their hatred. Their only grievance against the believers was their faith in Allah, the Almighty and Praiseworthy, who alone possesses the sovereignty of the heavens and the earth. This highlights that oppression often stems from the disbelievers' intolerance of faith, not from any wrongdoing by the believers.

Ayah 10-11
Fate of the Persecutors

A stern warning is given to those who oppress the believers: unless they repent, they will face the torment of Hell, a punishment of intense burning. In contrast, those who remain steadfast in faith and righteousness will be rewarded with Gardens beneath which rivers flow. This contrast emphasises the ultimate victory of faith over oppression, where patience and belief lead to eternal success.

Ayah 12-16
Absolute Power and Mercy of Allah

The punishment of Allah is described as severe, reminding that He alone begins creation and repeats it, reinforcing His ability to resurrect and judge. Yet, alongside His might, He is also Forgiving and Loving, showing that those who repent can still find mercy. Allah, the Possessor of the Glorious Throne, does whatever He wills, demonstrating His unmatched authority and control over all affairs.

Ayah 17-20
Warnings from Pharaoh & Thamood

The Quran reminds the audience of past nations who defied Allah's messengers, particularly Pharaoh and Thamood. Their arrogance led to their destruction, serving as a lesson that disbelief and injustice inevitably lead to downfall. The disbelievers remain in denial, despite clear signs, but they cannot escape Allah's grasp, as He encloses them from all sides, ensuring that justice will be served.

Ayah 21-22
Glorious Nature of the Quran

The chapter concludes by affirming the Quran's divine origin. It is a Glorious Quran, not an ordinary speech, but one preserved in a Preserved Tablet (al-Lawh al-Mahfuz), signifying its protection from corruption. This serves as a reassurance that Allah's message remains untouched and will guide humanity until the end of time.

Lessons to Learn

- Oppression against believers will be avenged by Allah.
- True faith requires patience and steadfastness, even in hardship.
- Allah's power is greater than any tyrant's rule.
- Past nations were destroyed for their arrogance; today's oppressors are no different.

Action Steps

- Remain firm in your faith, even in difficult times.
- Support and stand up for oppressed believers worldwide.
- Trust that Allah's justice will be served, even if it seems delayed.
- Read and reflect on the Qur'an regularly, as it is the eternal truth.

Revealed in	Juz	Surah No.	No. of verses
Makkah	30	86	17

سُورَةُ الطَّارِقِ

SURAH AT-TARIQ

(THE NIGHT VISITOR)

يَوْمَ تُبْلَى ٱلسَّرَآئِرُ ۝ فَمَا لَهُۥ مِن قُوَّةٍ وَلَا نَاصِرٍ ۝

"On the Day all secrets will be disclosed. Then one will have neither power nor 'any' helper." (86:9-10)

Context

This Surah was revealed during a time when the Quraysh were rejecting the message of resurrection and accountability. It addresses human arrogance by reminding them of their humble origins—created from a mere drop of fluid—& asserts Allah's power to resurrect. The Surah also warns that all hidden intentions and secrets will be exposed on the Day of Judgement.

Topics

- Oath by the Night Star (Tariq)
- Creation of Man
- Allah's Power to Resurrect Mankind
- Exposure of all Secrets on Judgement Day
- The Qur'an as a Decisive Truth

Theme

Surah At-Tariq emphasises Allah's supreme power over creation, resurrection, & accountability. It begins with an oath by the piercing star to affirm the reality of the Hereafter. The Surah highlights the vulnerability of humans, who were created from a mere drop of fluid, & reminds them that Allah can bring them back to life. The Surah also warns that all hidden deeds will be exposed, & no power can protect the disbelievers from divine judgement.

Virtues & Benefits

This Surah strengthens your faith in resurrection & accountability. It also emphasises Allah's power in creation & the Hereafter. Also it encourages self-reflection, as all secrets will be exposed.

Ayah 1-3

The Oath by the Sky

Allah begins by swearing by the sky and at-Tariq, a mysterious entity whose significance is questioned and then revealed—it is the Piercing Star. This celestial body is described as something striking and radiant, symbolizing guidance in the darkness. The mention of this star emphasizes Allah's power in creation and serves as a metaphor for divine revelation cutting through ignorance.

Ayah 4-7

Reality of Human Creation

Allah reminds humans that each soul has a divine protector watching over it. This highlights His complete knowledge and control over all affairs. The passage then calls on humans to reflect on their origins—created from a gushing fluid that comes from between the backbone and breastbones. This is a humbling reminder of human fragility, reinforcing the idea that life is not self-sustaining but entirely dependent on Allah's will.

Ayah 8-10

Unveiling of Secrets

Allah affirms His ability to resurrect human beings. The Day of Judgment will be a time when all hidden matters—actions, thoughts, and intentions—will be exposed. On that day, people will stand powerless, without any strength or supporters to defend them. This serves as a warning that no worldly power can prevent divine justice from taking its course.

Ayah 11-14

Truth of Revelation

The sky is described as something that "returns," which can refer to its role in sending down rain, sustaining life on Earth. The Earth, in turn, cracks open to allow plants to grow, demonstrating cycles of life, death, and rebirth—echoing the concept of resurrection. Allah then asserts that the Quran is a Decisive Word—a truth that is not to be taken lightly or dismissed as a mere jest.

Ayah 15-16

Scheming of Disbelievers

The disbelievers engage in plotting and scheming against the truth, whether by opposing the Prophet ﷺ or attempting to distort Allah's message. However, Allah makes it clear that He, too, has His own divine plan, one that will ultimately overpower and render their schemes ineffective. This highlights that no matter how much people try to resist the truth, Allah's will prevails.

Ayah 17

Temporary Respite for Disbelievers

Allah instructs the Prophet ﷺ to grant the disbelievers a brief respite. This implies that their time is limited, and even though they may seem victorious in the short term, their fate is sealed. This verse serves as both a warning to them and reassurance to the believers that divine justice will eventually take place.

Lessons to Learn

- Allah's signs in the universe affirm His power and wisdom.
- Humans should not be arrogant, as they were created from a mere drop of fluid.
- Nothing is hidden from Allah; every secret will be revealed.
- The Qur'an is a clear and decisive message from Allah.

Action Steps

- Reflect on Allah's creation as proof of His power.
- Strengthen your belief in the Hereafter and accountability.
- Avoid arrogance; remember your humble origins.
- Be mindful of your intentions and actions, as nothing is hidden from Allah.

Revealed in	Juz	Surah No.	No. of verses
Makkah	30	87	19

سُورَةُ الأَعْلَىٰ

SURAH AL-A'LA

(THE MOST HIGH)

فَذَكِّرْ إِن نَّفَعَتِ ٱلذِّكْرَىٰ ۝ سَيَذَّكَّرُ مَن يَخْشَىٰ ۝

"So 'always' remind 'with the Quran'—'even' if the reminder is beneficial 'only to some'. Those in awe 'of Allah' will be mindful 'of it'." (87: 9-10)

Context

The Surah was revealed to remind the Prophet ﷺ and the believers to remember and praise Allah for His greatness and the blessings He has provided. It emphasises Allah's creation, His power, and the importance of submission to Him.

Topics

- The Greatness of Allah's Creation
- The Importance of Glorifying Allah
- Signs of Allah in Nature
- Guidance Allah Provides to His Servants

Theme

The Surah emphasises Allah's supremacy and power over all creation. It reminds humans of the greatness of Allah, urging them to praise and submit to Him. The Surah describes Allah's creative power and the signs of His majesty found in nature, calling believers to remember Him in gratitude and faith.

Virtues & Benefits

Reciting this Surah brings tranquility to the heart and strengthens the connection with Allah. It is a Surah of high praise, reminding believers of Allah's power and majesty, which fosters humility.

Ayah 1-5
The Majesty of Allah's Creation

The chapter begins with a call to glorify and praise Allah, the Most High. He is the Creator who not only brings things into existence but also organizes and regulates them with perfect precision. Every living thing is created with a purpose and guided toward its function. Allah produces lush green pastures, but in time, they wither and turn into dry, scattered debris. This serves as a reminder of the fleeting nature of worldly life and the power of Allah over all creation.

Ayah 6-8
The Prophet's ﷺ Guidance

Allah reassures the Prophet Muhammad ﷺ that He will help him retain the revelation and that he will not forget it, except in what Allah wills. This highlights divine wisdom—some matters are revealed at the right time, while others remain hidden. Allah knows everything, both what is openly declared and what remains concealed in the hearts. The Prophet is further assured that his mission will be made easy for him, emphasizing that Islam is a path of ease and balance.

Ayah 9-13
The Fate of the Reverent

The Prophet ﷺ is encouraged to remind people of the truth, for those who fear Allah will take heed. However, the wretched—those who persist in their arrogance and disbelief—will turn away from the message. Their fate is the Gigantic Fire, where they will neither find relief in death nor true life, but rather, continuous suffering. This serves as a dire warning about the consequences of rejecting faith.

Ayah 14-15
The Path to Success

True success lies in self-purification—both spiritually and morally. Those who cleanse their souls, remember Allah, and remain steadfast in prayer are the ones who will be truly victorious. This highlights the fundamental acts of worship in Islam, which serve as a means to elevate the soul and attain Allah's pleasure.

Ayah 16-17
The Illusion of This World

Many people prioritize the fleeting pleasures of this world over the eternal blessings of the Hereafter. However, Allah reminds us that the Hereafter is far superior and everlasting. The worldly life is temporary, but the rewards and punishments of the Hereafter are permanent. This verse urges believers to shift their focus toward what truly matters.

Ayah 18-19
The Message in Previous Scriptures

The teachings of this chapter are not new; they were also revealed in the scriptures of Ibrahim and Musa (AS). This reinforces the continuity of divine guidance throughout history. The message of Tawheed (the oneness of Allah) and righteousness remains unchanged, emphasizing that Islam is a continuation of the same truth revealed to earlier prophets.

Lessons to Learn

- Always remember Allah and reflect upon His signs.
- Understand the consequences of heedlessness and disbelief.
- Strive for spiritual success by remaining faithful and obedient to Allah.
- Accept the guidance provided by Allah through His prophets.

Action Steps

- Begin each day by reflecting on Allah's blessings and power.
- Make a habit of remembering Allah throughout the day, through dhikr and contemplation.
- Strive to implement the teachings of the Qur'an in daily actions and interactions with others.
- Regularly recite Surah Al-Ala to strengthen your faith

Revealed in	Juz	Surah No.	No. of verses
Makkah	30	88	26

سُورَةُ الغَاشِيَةِ

SURAH AL-GHASHIYAH

(THE OVERWHELMING)

إِنَّ إِلَيْنَآ إِيَابَهُمْ ۝ ثُمَّ إِنَّ عَلَيْنَا حِسَابَهُم ۝

"Surely to Us is their return, then surely with Us is their reckoning." (88:25-26)

Context

This Surah was revealed to describe the fate of those who reject Allah's message and the stark contrast between the end of the disbelievers and the believers. It paints vivid imagery of the Day of Judgement to warn people and encourage them to reflect upon the consequences of their choices.

Topics

- The Fate of the Disbelievers
- The Bliss of the Righteous
- Descriptions of the Day of Judgement
- The Signs of Allah in Creation
- Overwhelming Nature of the Day of Judgement

Theme

Surah Al-Ghashiya focuses on the events of the Day of Judgement. It contrasts the fates of the disbelievers, who will face overwhelming punishment, and the believers, who will experience peace and reward. The Surah serves as a reminder of the consequences of one's actions and the certainty of the afterlife.

Virtues & Benefits

Reciting this Surah reminds us of the importance of accountability in the Hereafter. It brings comfort to the believers, knowing that their efforts to follow Allah's guidance will be rewarded.

Ayah 1-7

The Fate of the Wretched

The chapter begins with a question meant to grab attention: Has the news of the overwhelming event reached you? This refers to the Day of Judgement, a day so intense and inescapable that it will overwhelm all of creation. On that day, some faces will reflect misery and humiliation, showing signs of exhaustion from their struggles in the worldly life—struggles that ultimately led them to ruin. Their punishment will be severe, as they are roasted in scorching fire and given burning water to drink. Their only food will be thorny plants, which neither provide nourishment nor satisfy their hunger. This scene serves as a stark warning about the consequences of disbelief and wrongdoing.

Ayah 8-16

The Reward of the Righteous

In contrast, other faces will be glowing with joy and contentment, pleased with their efforts in the world. These are the believers who lived righteous lives and will now reap the rewards of their faith. They will reside in an elevated paradise, free from all nonsense and hardship. The passage describes their luxurious surroundings—flowing springs, raised beds, elegant cups, rows of cushions, and beautifully spread carpets. This imagery highlights the immense comfort and peace that await the righteous, contrasting with the suffering of those doomed to Hell.

Ayah 17-20

Signs of Divine Power in Creation

Allah then calls upon humans to reflect on His creation. The camel is mentioned as a remarkable creature, perfectly designed for its environment. The sky, raised high without visible pillars, the mountains, firmly fixed in place, and the earth, spread out for human habitation—all serve as signs of Allah's mastery and wisdom. These verses encourage contemplation of the natural world as proof of divine power, urging people to recognize the reality of the Hereafter.

Ayah 21-22

The Prophet's Role as a Reminder

The Prophet Muhammad ﷺ is reassured that his duty is simply to remind people of the truth. He is not responsible for forcing belief upon them, nor does he have control over their choices. This highlights a key principle in Islam—that guidance is ultimately in Allah's hands, and the role of a messenger is only to deliver the message.

Ayah 23-24

The Consequence of Rejection

For those who turn away and reject the message, a severe punishment awaits. This punishment is described as the greatest punishment, indicating that nothing in this world can compare to the suffering of the Hereafter. The warning serves as a final call for reflection and repentance before it is too late.

Ayah 25-26

Ultimate Return & Reckoning

The chapter concludes with a powerful reminder: all humans will ultimately return to Allah. It is He alone who will judge them and hold them accountable for their actions. This serves as both a warning to wrongdoers and a reassurance to the righteous, emphasising that divine justice will be fulfilled without any injustice.

Lessons to Learn

- The consequences of neglecting Allah's guidance are severe and overwhelming, urging believers to remain vigilant.
- The rewards of the righteous are beyond imagination and serve as a great motivation for perseverance in faith.
- Reflecting on the signs of Allah in the world around us helps strengthen our faith and understanding.

Action Steps

- Take time daily to reflect on the signs of Allah's creation, strengthening your faith and gratitude.
- Keep the reality of the afterlife in mind when making decisions, ensuring that your actions align with Islamic principles.
- Regularly recite Surah Al-Ghashiya to remind yourself of the rewards and consequences associated with the afterlife.

Revealed in	Juz	Surah No.	No. of verses
Makkah	30	89	30

سُورَةُ الفَجْرِ

SURAH AL-FAJR

(THE DAWN)

يَـٰٓأَيَّتُهَا ٱلنَّفْسُ ٱلْمُطْمَئِنَّةُ ۝ ٱرْجِعِىٓ إِلَىٰ رَبِّكِ رَاضِيَةً مَّرْضِيَّةً ۝ فَٱدْخُلِى فِى
عِبَـٰدِى ۝ وَٱدْخُلِى جَنَّتِى ۝

"'Allah will say to the righteous,' "O tranquil soul! Return to your Lord, well pleased 'with Him' and well pleasing 'to Him'. So join My servants, and enter My Paradise." (89:27-30)

Context

The Surah was revealed to remind people of the inevitable Day of Judgement and the fate of previous nations who were destroyed for their disbelief and sinful ways. It emphasises Allah's ability to bring about justice, rewarding the righteous and punishing the wicked, urging reflection on one's actions in this life.

Topics

- The Day of Judgement
- The Fate of Previous Nations
- Allah's Power and Justice
- The Contrast Between the Fate of the Righteous and the Wicked
- The Signs of Allah in Creation

Theme

Surah Al-Fajr highlights the grandeur of Allah's power and the certainty of the Day of Judgement. It serves as a reminder of the consequences faced by those who reject faith and live in arrogance, as well as the rewards awaiting the righteous. The Surah also encourages reflection on Allah's signs in creation and the lessons from past nations.

Virtues & Benefits

Reciting Surah Al-Fajr brings spiritual clarity and a reminder of the Day of Judgement. It serves as a powerful reminder to reflect on one's actions, both good and bad, and work towards righteousness.

Ayah 1-5
The Oath and Its Significance

Allah begins by swearing by powerful natural and cosmic signs—daybreak, ten nights (often interpreted as the first ten days of Dhul-Hijjah), the even and the odd, and the receding night. These oaths draw attention to the cycles of time and the divine order in creation. The final verse in this section asks whether these signs are enough for a rational person to reflect upon, emphasizing the importance of wisdom and contemplation.

Ayah 6-14
The Fate of Past Nations

Allah reminds us of the destruction of powerful civilizations—Aad, known for their mighty structures; Erum, which was unmatched in grandeur; Thamood, who carved homes into solid rock; and Pharaoh, infamous for his tyranny. Despite their strength, they were destroyed for their arrogance and corruption. This serves as a warning that no power can stand against divine justice, and Allah is always watching over the actions of humanity.

Ayah 15-21
Misconceptions of Wealth & Honour

Many people wrongly believe that wealth and prosperity are signs of divine favor, while hardship and poverty are signs of disgrace. Allah refutes this misconception, stating that true honor comes from righteousness, not material success. He then highlights human neglect of moral duties—failing to care for orphans, refusing to help the poor, and obsessing over wealth. This section serves as a reminder that true success is measured by generosity and righteousness, not material possessions.

Ayah 21-23
The Terror of the Day of Judgment

A terrifying scene of the Last Day is described—when the earth is crushed and levelled, and Allah arrives with rows of angels. Hell itself will be brought forward as a stark reality for those who denied the truth. At that moment, people will desperately wish they had prepared for this day, but their regret will be of no use. This passage serves as a powerful reminder that one's actions in this world determine their fate in the Hereafter.

Ayah 24-26
Punishment of the Disbelievers

On that Day, no one can punish as Allah punishes, and no one can bind as He binds. This emphasises the severity of divine justice for those who led lives of defiance and arrogance. Their rejection of faith and morality will lead them to consequences beyond human comprehension. The finality of divine punishment makes it clear that no one can escape the consequences of their deeds.

Ayah 27-30
The Reward for the Righteous

In contrast, the righteous are addressed with beautiful words: O tranquil soul. These are the believers who lived a life of faith and righteousness, now invited to return to their Lord in peace. They will be counted among Allah's honoured servants and granted eternal entry into Paradise. This passage highlights the ultimate goal of the believer—a state of peace, acceptance, and everlasting joy in the presence of Allah.

Lessons to Learn

- Allah's justice is certain and inevitable; both the righteous and the wicked will be judged fairly.
- Reflecting on the fate of past nations can help us learn from their mistakes and avoid arrogance and sin.
- The Day of Judgement is a reminder that our actions in this life determine our fate in the hereafter.

Action Steps

- Start each day with gratitude for Allah's blessings and reflect on how to use your time wisely.
- Regularly recite Surah Al-Fajr, especially during the early morning or at night, as a reminder of the afterlife.
- Avoid arrogance and heedlessness by remaining humble, grateful, and conscious of Allah's guidance.

Revealed in	Juz	Surah No.	No. of verses
Makkah	30	90	20

سُورَةُ البَلَدِ

SURAH AL-BALAD

(THE CITY)

ثُمَّ كَانَ مِنَ ٱلَّذِينَ ءَامَنُوا۟ وَتَوَاصَوْا۟ بِٱلصَّبْرِ وَتَوَاصَوْا۟ بِٱلْمَرْحَمَةِ ۞ أُو۟لَٰٓئِكَ أَصْحَٰبُ ٱلْمَيْمَنَةِ ۞

"and—above all—to be one of those who have faith and urge each other to perseverance and urge each other to compassion. These are the people of the right." (90:17-18)

Context

The Surah was revealed to emphasise the challenges and difficulties that human beings face in life, and the choices they make. It calls people to righteousness, urging them to serve others, especially the needy. It stresses that true success is found in helping others and living in accordance with Allah's commands.

Topics

- Challenges of Human Life
- City of Makkah as a Significant Place
- Human Arrogance
- The Contrast Between the Righteous and the Selfish
- Need to Strive for Righteousness

Theme

Surah Al-Balad highlights the struggle of human life and the moral challenges faced by individuals. It calls people to reflect on their purpose in life and the choices they make. The Surah emphasises that true success lies not in material wealth but in helping those in need and seeking Allah's approval through righteous deeds.

Virtues & Benefits

Reciting Surah Al-Balad reminds us of the challenges & responsibilities in life & encourages reflection on our purpose. It promotes charity and empathy towards those in need.

Ayah 1-3
The Oath by the Sacred Land

Allah begins with an oath by the land, referring to Makkah, a place of immense spiritual and historical significance. The mention of the Prophet's residence in this land emphasises his connection to it and the importance of the message being revealed there. Additionally, the mention of a father and what he fathered signifies lineage, creation, and the continuation of human generations, reminding us of Allah's divine order in human existence.

Ayah 4-7
The Trials of Human Life

Humans are created in a state of hardship and struggle, emphasising that life is full of challenges meant to test patience and faith. However, many people, instead of recognising their dependence on Allah, become arrogant. They boast about their wealth and assume no one has control over them, forgetting that Allah sees and knows all their actions. This serves as a reminder that material possessions do not define success, and accountability is inevitable.

Ayah 8-10
The Blessings of Guidance

Allah reminds humans of the gifts He has given them—eyes, a tongue, lips, and the ability to distinguish between right and wrong. These blessings are meant to guide them towards righteousness, but it is up to each individual to use them wisely. The mention of the two ways refers to the path of righteousness and the path of misguidance, highlighting the personal responsibility each person has in choosing their direction in life.

Ayah 11-16
The Ascent to True Righteousness

Many people fail to take the ascent, which represents the difficult yet rewarding path of righteousness. Allah clarifies what this ascent entails—acts of compassion such as freeing slaves, feeding the hungry, & caring for orphans & the poor. These acts require selflessness and sacrifice, demonstrating that true righteousness is not just about belief but also about social responsibility and helping those in need.

Ayah 17-18
The People of Happiness

True believers are not only those who have faith but also those who practice patience and kindness, encouraging others to do the same. These are the qualities that define the people of happiness, meaning those who will attain eternal success in the Hereafter. Their actions reflect their sincerity, and they are rewarded with lasting peace and joy.

Ayah 19-20
The People of Misery

In contrast, those who reject Allah's signs and live in defiance are labelled the people of misery. Their fate is sealed in a padlocked Fire, meaning a punishment from which there is no escape. This stark warning serves as a reminder that arrogance and selfishness lead to destruction, whereas faith and compassion lead to eternal happiness.

Lessons to Learn

- Life is full of struggles and challenges, but we are responsible for how we respond to them.
- Helping others, especially those in need, is one of the most significant ways to earn Allah's favour.
- True success is not defined by material wealth, but by moral integrity, compassion, and good deeds.

Action Steps

- Reflect on the challenges you face and choose to respond with patience, faith, and perseverance.
- Actively seek opportunities to help those in need, whether through charity, volunteer work, or small acts of kindness.
- Prioritise moral actions over material gain, focusing on the spiritual rewards that come from serving others.

Revealed in	Juz	Surah No.	No. of verses
Makkah	30	91	15

سُورَةُ الشَّمْسِ

SURAH ASH-SHAMS

(THE SUN)

قَدْ أَفْلَحَ مَن زَكَّىٰهَا ۝ وَقَدْ خَابَ مَن دَسَّىٰهَا ۝

"Successful indeed is the one who purifies their soul, and doomed is the one who corrupts it!"
(91:9-10)

Context

The Surah was revealed to emphasise the creation of Allah and the balance of nature as signs of His power. It highlights the role of the human soul in choosing between righteousness and sin. It underscores the internal struggle and how one's deeds shape their destiny, warning against following the path of corruption and sin.

Topics

- World as Signs of Allah's Power
- Contrast Between the Pure and Corrupt Soul
- The Role of Self-Purification
- The Consequences of Ignoring Righteousness

Theme

Surah Ash-Shams reflects on the greatness of Allah's creation, particularly the sun, as a sign of His power and order. The Surah contrasts the pure soul (nafs) that seeks righteousness with the corrupt soul that leads to destruction. It stresses the importance of purifying the soul to achieve success and warns of the consequences of corruption.

Virtues & Benefits

Reciting Surah Ash-Shams helps instil a sense of reflection on one's soul and encourages self-purification. It serves as a reminder of the balance in Allah's creation.

Ayah 1-6

Cosmic Oath and Divine Order

This passage begins with a series of oaths by celestial and natural elements—the sun, moon, day, night, sky, and earth. Each of these plays a vital role in maintaining balance in the universe. The contrast between light & darkness, revelation & concealment, symbolises the choices humans make between guidance and misguidance. These verses highlight Allah's perfect design, reminding humanity of His power and control over all existence.

Ayah 7-8

Perfection of the Human Soul

Just as Allah has perfectly created the physical world, He has also fashioned the human soul with precision. He has given it the capacity to recognise both righteousness and wickedness. Every person is equipped with a moral compass, an inner sense of right and wrong, and the ability to choose their path. This emphasises human responsibility in shaping their destiny based on the choices they make.

Ayah 9-10

Formula for Success and Failure

Success is promised to those who nurture and purify their souls by engaging in righteousness, faith, and self-discipline. On the other hand, failure awaits those who neglect and corrupt their souls through sin, arrogance, and rejection of guidance. This serves as a powerful reminder that true success is not measured by worldly gains but by one's spiritual and moral integrity.

Ayah 11-12

Arrogance of the People of Thamood

The passage then shifts to the historical example of the Thamood people, who were given clear signs from Allah but chose pride and defiance instead of faith. They refused to acknowledge the truth despite being warned, demonstrating how arrogance can lead people away from righteousness. Their downfall serves as a lesson for all generations about the consequences of rejecting divine guidance.

Ayah 13-14

She-Camel as a Divine Test

The people of Thamood were given a miraculous sign—a she-camel sent by Allah as a test of their obedience. The Prophet sent to them warned that they should not harm it and allow it to drink freely. However, their rejection of faith led them to commit a great sin by killing the she-camel, an act that sealed their fate. This event highlights how those who deny clear signs of Allah often go to extreme lengths in their defiance.

Ayah 15

Destruction of Thamood

As a result of their transgression, Allah's punishment descended upon them, completely destroying their civilisation. Their arrogance and defiance could not save them from divine justice. The passage concludes by affirming that Allah does not fear the consequences of His judgement, for His decisions are based on absolute wisdom and justice. This final statement reinforces that no force can challenge Allah's will, and those who reject His guidance will inevitably face the consequences.

Lessons to Learn

- The soul is capable of both great purity and corruption; the choice is ours to make.
- Allah has given humans the ability to discern right from wrong, making them responsible for their actions.
- Purification of the soul is the key to success, and it involves seeking righteousness, self-control, and devotion to Allah.

Action Steps

- Regularly reflect on your actions and intentions, aiming for self-purification and improvement.
- Avoid arrogance and corruption by staying humble, seeking righteousness, and striving for moral integrity.
- Perform acts of charity and goodness, which help purify the soul and strengthen the connection with Allah.

Revealed in	Juz	Surah No.	No. of verses
Makkah	30	92	21

سُورَةُ اللَّيْلِ

SURAH AL-LAYL

(THE NIGHT)

فَأَمَّا مَنْ أَعْطَىٰ وَٱتَّقَىٰ ۝ وَصَدَّقَ بِٱلْحُسْنَىٰ ۝ فَسَنُيَسِّرُهُۥ لِلْيُسْرَىٰ ۝

"As for the one who is charitable, mindful 'of Allah', and 'firmly' believes in the finest reward, We will facilitate for them the Way of Ease." (92:5-7)

Context

This Surah was revealed to highlight the contrasting forces of good and evil in human life, symbolised by the night and the day. It speaks of the choices people make, how actions lead to either success or failure, and the consequences of their choices. It encourages the believer to choose the path of righteousness.

Topics

- The Contrast Between Good & Evil
- Personal Effort in Achieving Success
- Righteousness as means to success
- Consequences of rejecting faith
- Power of Allah in Determining Outcomes

Theme

Surah Al-Lail contrasts the different paths people choose in life, symbolised by the darkness of the night and the light of the day. It illustrates that those who choose righteousness and give in charity will be rewarded, while those who reject faith and live selfishly will face destruction. It stresses the role of individual choices in shaping one's destiny.

Virtues & Benefits

Reciting Surah Al-Lail helps foster reflection on one's choices, reminding the believer of the consequences of actions in both this life and the Hereafter. It encourages acts of good deeds.

Ayah 1-3

Oath by Night and Day

Allah begins with an oath by the night as it covers and the day as it reveals. Night symbolises darkness, rest, and concealment, while day represents light, action, and clarity. These opposites illustrate the duality of life—hardship and ease, struggle and relief. The mention of "He who created the male and the female" further emphasises the theme of balance and pairs in creation, showing Allah's perfect design in all things.

Ayah 4-7

The Contrast Between Paths

Allah states: "Your endeavours are indeed diverse." This means that people take different paths in life—some choose righteousness, while others choose selfishness. Those who "give and are righteous" and "confirm goodness" will find their way made easy towards ease, meaning success in both this world and the Hereafter. This verse encourages generosity, faith, and positive action, reassuring that those who do good will find life's journey facilitated by Allah.

Ayah 8-11

Consequence of Stinginess

In contrast, the one who is "stingy and complacent" and "denies goodness" will find their path eased towards difficulty. Those who withhold charity, ignore righteousness, and reject faith will face increasing hardship. Their wealth, which they relied on, will not avail them when they plummet, material possessions will be useless in the face of divine judgement. These verses serve as a warning that rejecting faith and generosity leads only to suffering.

Ayah 12-13

Authority Belongs to Allah

Allah declares: "It is upon Us to guide." This affirms that true guidance comes from Him alone. Additionally, "To Us belong the Last and the First" emphasises that Allah is the Master of both this world and the Hereafter. This reminds believers to trust in Allah's plan and seek His guidance, as He alone controls destiny.

Ayah 14-16

The Warning of the Fire

Allah warns of "a Fierce Blaze" that awaits "the very wicked." This punishment is reserved for those who "deny and turn away" from faith and righteousness. These verses serve as a severe reminder that rejecting Allah's guidance has dire consequences, urging people to reflect on their choices and avoid the path of disbelief.

Ayah 17-21

Reward of the Righteous

In contrast, "the devout will avoid it"—those who are generous and seek purification through charity will be saved. The righteous give "seeking no favour in return" but only for "the acceptance of his Lord, the Most High." This selfless devotion ensures that they will attain ultimate satisfaction in the Hereafter. The passage ends with a beautiful promise: "And he will be satisfied"—meaning Allah will grant true fulfilment and eternal reward to those who sincerely seek Him.

Lessons to Learn

- Life is shaped by the choices we make; each action has a consequence, whether good or bad.
- Righteousness, charity, and helping others lead to success in both this life and the Hereafter.
- Selfishness and rejection of faith lead to destruction and loss, both in this world and the next.

Action Steps

- Reflect on your actions daily, and strive to choose the path of charity, kindness, and righteousness.
- Avoid selfishness and hoarding; instead, help those in need and contribute to the welfare of others.
- Regularly engage in acts of worship and good deeds, keeping the intention of pleasing Allah.

Revealed in	Juz	Surah No.	No. of verses
Makkah	30	93	11

سُورَةُ الضُّحَىٰ

SURAH AD-DUHAA

(THE MORNING BRIGHTNESS)

وَأَمَّا بِنِعْمَةِ رَبِّكَ فَحَدِّثْ ۝

"And proclaim the blessings of your Lord." (93:11)

Context

The Surah was revealed to console and reassure the Prophet Muhammad ﷺ during a period of distress, where there was a brief pause in revelation. It was a time of emotional difficulty for him, and this Surah emphasises Allah's continual support, reminding him of past blessings and assuring him that his future will be better than the past.

Topics

- Comfort During Times of Hardship
- Allah's Continuous Blessings
- Importance of Charity
- Encouragement for the Prophet ﷺ to Continue His Mission With Perseverance and Faith

Theme

Surah Ad-Dhuha is about reassurance and hope. It reminds the Prophet ﷺ that Allah has never abandoned him and that brighter days are ahead. The Surah emphasises Allah's mercy, reminding the Prophet ﷺ of His past blessings, and calls for gratitude and continued effort in helping others, particularly the poor and needy.

Virtues & Benefits

Reciting Surah Ad-Dhuha brings relief during times of hardship & reminds the believer that Allah's mercy & support are always near. It emphasises hope & the belief that difficulties are temporary.

Ayah 1-2

Oath by Morning and Night

Allah begins with an oath by the morning light and the night as it settles. The morning symbolises hope, renewal, and guidance, while the night represents difficulties, trials, & uncertainty. By swearing upon these contrasting times, Allah reassures the Prophet Muhammad ﷺ that just as night is followed by morning, hardship will be followed by ease. This serves as a universal message of optimism for all believers facing struggles.

Ayah 3

Reassurance of Allah's Presence

Allah directly comforts the Prophet ﷺ by declaring: "Your Lord did not abandon you, nor did He forget." This verse addresses a moment when the Prophet ﷺ felt sorrow due to a temporary pause in revelation. Allah affirms that He is always near and attentive. This reminder extends to all believers—no matter how difficult life gets, Allah never forsakes His servants.

Ayah 4-5

Promise of a Better Future

Allah assures that "the Hereafter is better for you than the First." This verse emphasises that the rewards of the afterlife far exceed the challenges of this world. Furthermore, Allah promises the Prophet ﷺ, "your Lord will give you, and you will be satisfied." This divine assurance applies not only to the Prophet ﷺ but also to all who trust in Allah's plan, reminding them that their patience and faith will be rewarded.

Ayah 6-8

Allah's Care and Guidance

Allah reminds the Prophet ﷺ of His past blessings, Allah protected the Prophet ﷺ despite his difficult childhood, Allah granted him spiritual guidance and wisdom. Allah provided sustenance and support.These verses highlight that Allah's help has always been present and will continue to be. They also serve as a reminder for all believers to reflect on their blessings, recognising Allah's care in their lives.

Ayah 9-10

Duty to Care for Others

In gratitude for Allah's generosity, believers are instructed, "Therefore, do not mistreat the orphan."—Since Allah cared for the Prophet ﷺ as an orphan, he must, in turn, show kindness to orphans. "Nor rebuff the seeker."—Whether someone seeks knowledge, help, or guidance, they should be treated with respect and generosity.These commands emphasise social responsibility, urging Muslims to show compassion to the vulnerable.

Ayah 11

Sharing Allah's Blessings

The passage concludes with the command: "But proclaim the blessings of your Lord." This means recognising and expressing gratitude for Allah's favours. Sharing blessings—whether through charity, kindness, or spreading knowledge—is a way of fulfilling this duty. This verse teaches that gratitude is not just an internal feeling but must be expressed through actions that benefit others.

Lessons to Learn

- Allah's mercy and support are constant, even in difficult times. Hardships are followed by ease, just as night is followed by day.
- Past difficulties should be viewed in the context of Allah's blessings, and His plan is always for the best.
- Gratitude, generosity, and charity are key components of a righteous life.

Action Steps

- Reflect on past blessings during times of hardship to understand how Allah's mercy has always been present.
- Engage in acts of charity to those in need, particularly orphans and the poor, as a way to express gratitude for Allah's blessings.
- Cultivate patience, knowing that difficulties are temporary, and trust that better days are ahead.

Revealed in	Juz	Surah No.	No. of verses
Makkah	30	94	8

سُورَةُ الشَّرْحِ

SURAH ASH-SHARH

(THE EXPANDING)

أَلَمْ نَشْرَحْ لَكَ صَدْرَكَ ۝ وَوَضَعْنَا عَنكَ وِزْرَكَ ۝ ٱلَّذِىٓ أَنقَضَ ظَهْرَكَ ۝

"Have We not uplifted your heart for you 'O Prophet', relieved you of the burden which weighed so heavily on your back," (94:1-3)

Context

This Surah was revealed during a time of difficulty for the Prophet Muhammad ﷺ, when he faced rejection and hardship from his people. The Surah reassures him, encouraging him to remain patient and steadfast. Allah reminds him of the relief He has already provided and that more ease and blessings will follow.

Topics

- Nature of Hardship and Ease
- Allah's Mercy & Relief After Difficulty
- Patience in the Face of Adversity
- Gratitude for Allah's Blessings & favour

Theme

Surah Al-Inshirah emphasises that after every hardship, there is relief. It provides comfort to the Prophet Muhammad ﷺ by reminding him that the difficulties he is experiencing will be followed by ease and blessings. The Surah stresses that patience in the face of trials will lead to success and that Allah is always there to provide support.

Virtues & Benefits

Reciting Surah Al-Inshirah brings comfort and relief during times of hardship. It encourages patience and trust in Allah, knowing that difficulties are temporary and will be followed by ease.

Ayah 1

Comfort & Reassurance from Allah

The passage begins with a rhetorical question: "Did We not soothe your heart?" This verse directly addresses the Prophet Muhammad ﷺ, reminding him of the divine support he has received. It highlights how Allah provides inner peace and spiritual strength, especially in times of difficulty. This reassurance is not only for the Prophet ﷺ but also for all believers facing challenges in life.

Ayah 2-3

The Removal of Burdens

These verses acknowledge the burdens that weighed heavily on the Prophet ﷺ, both physically and emotionally. The phrase "which weighed down your back" symbolizes immense struggles, hardships, and responsibilities. Allah's intervention in lifting these burdens signifies His continuous mercy, showing that He provides relief to those who endure hardships with patience and faith.

Ayah 4

The Elevation of Honour

Allah reminds the Prophet ﷺ of how his status and reputation were elevated. From being an orphan and facing rejection, he was chosen as the final messenger, his name being honored throughout history. This verse reassures that when one follows the path of righteousness, divine support leads to elevation and success, regardless of initial struggles.

Ayah 5-6

Promise of Ease After Hardship

The repetition of "With hardship comes ease" emphasizes a fundamental truth of life—every struggle is accompanied by relief. The repetition serves to reassure believers that no difficulty is permanent and that divine help always follows hardships. This principle encourages patience and perseverance, knowing that Allah's mercy is near.

Ayah 7

Devotion After Completing Duties

Once worldly responsibilities are fulfilled, the verse instructs believers to "turn to devotion." This means that after finishing one's daily tasks, a person should dedicate time to worship and spiritual growth. It highlights the importance of balancing work and faith, ensuring that one remains connected to Allah despite life's demands.

Ayah 8

Reliance on Allah in All Matters

The passage concludes with the ultimate lesson: "And to your Lord turn for everything." This verse emphasises complete reliance on Allah. No matter the challenges, triumphs, or uncertainties in life, true peace and success come from seeking closeness to Him. It serves as a final reminder that faith, patience, and devotion are the keys to overcoming life's struggles.

Lessons to Learn

- Every hardship is followed by ease, and relief from Allah comes after difficulty.
- Patience, perseverance, and continued effort are key to overcoming challenges.
- Turning to Allah in gratitude, especially in times of ease, strengthens our relationship with Him.

Action Steps

- When facing hardship, remind yourself that Allah's relief is near and that challenges are temporary.
- Practice patience and perseverance in every endeavour, knowing that ease will follow.
- Increase your gratitude for Allah's blessings, particularly during times of ease.

Revealed in	Juz	Surah No.	No. of verses
Makkah	30	95	8

سُورَةُ التِّينِ

SURAH AT-TIN

(THE FIG)

لَقَدْ خَلَقْنَا ٱلْإِنسَـٰنَ فِىٓ أَحْسَنِ تَقْوِيمٍ ۞ ثُمَّ رَدَدْنَـٰهُ أَسْفَلَ سَـٰفِلِينَ ۞ إِلَّا ٱلَّذِينَ
ءَامَنُوا۟ وَعَمِلُوا۟ ٱلصَّـٰلِحَـٰتِ فَلَهُمْ أَجْرٌ غَيْرُ مَمْنُونٍ ۞

"Indeed, We created humans in the best form. But We will reduce them to the lowest of the low 'in Hell', except those who believe and do good—they will have a never-ending reward." (95:4-6)

Context

The Surah was revealed to emphasise the importance of human nature and the potential for growth and corruption in every individual. It uses the imagery of the fig tree and the olive, which are symbolic of blessings, purity, and the potential for goodness in human beings. The Surah urges people to recognise their true potential and the consequences of their actions.

Topics

- The Creation of Man
- The Decline of Humanity
- The Role of Religion
- The Final Outcome

Theme

Surah At-Tin reflects on the inherent goodness & potential within humanity, using the metaphor of the fig and olive to represent righteousness & virtue. It highlights that humans are created with a noble nature but can be corrupted if they deviate from the path of righteousness. Ultimately, it stresses the importance of following the righteous path and seeking Allah's favor.

Virtues & Benefits

Reciting Surah At-Tin regularly helps to reflect on the true nature of humanity & the potential for both goodness & corruption. The Surah encourages moral integrity & the pursuit of righteousness.

Ayah 1-3

The Oath by Sacred Symbols

These verses begin with an oath by the fig & the olive, Mount Sinai, & this safe land (interpreted as Mecca). These elements symbolise places of spiritual significance. The fig & olive may represent regions associated with past prophets, Mount Sinai is where Musa (AS) received revelation, & the safe land refers to Mecca, the sanctuary of divine guidance. By swearing upon these sacred signs, the verses emphasise the truth & importance of the message that follows.

Ayah 4

The Excellence of Humans

This verse declares that Allah created man in "the best design." This signifies not only physical perfection but also the human capacity for intelligence, morality, and spiritual elevation. It reflects Allah 's wisdom in granting humans a noble status, with the ability to distinguish right from wrong and achieve great heights through faith and righteousness.

Ayah 5

The Potential for Degradation

Despite being created in the best form, humans can fall "to the lowest of the low." This refers to moral and spiritual decline when people abandon righteousness and give in to sinful behaviour. The verse highlights the consequences of turning away from Allah`s guidance—without faith and virtue, humans can become lower than even the simplest creatures in terms of their morality and purpose.

Ayah 6

The Exception for the Righteous

Not all people are doomed to such a fall. Those who maintain their faith and engage in righteous deeds are promised "a reward without end." This eternal reward refers to paradise, emphasising that belief and good actions elevate a person rather than degrade them. This verse reassures believers that their efforts in faith will not be in vain but will lead to everlasting success.

Ayah 7

The Challenge to the Disbelievers

After establishing the truth of human creation and divine justice, the verse challenges those who reject faith: "So why do you still reject the religion?" This question urges reflection—if humans are created with wisdom, given guidance, and promised eternal reward for righteousness, what reason remains for denying faith? It is a call to reconsider one's beliefs and recognise the truth.

Ayah 8

The Ultimate Wisdom of Allah

The passage concludes with a rhetorical question: "Is God not the Wisest of the wise?" This serves as a final reminder that everything in creation follows divine wisdom. The perfection of human design, the consequences of righteousness and sin, and the unfolding of divine justice all point to Allah`s ultimate wisdom. It leaves the reader with the undeniable truth that Allah`s knowledge and judgement surpass all human understanding.

Lessons to Learn

- Humans are created in the best of forms, and their potential for goodness is immense when they follow Allah's guidance.
- Moral & spiritual degradation occurs when individuals deviate from righteousness, and they are accountable for their actions.
- The promise of reward for those who remain righteous is a source of motivation for self-improvement and good conduct.

Action Steps

- Reflect on the blessings of creation and strive to live up to the noble potential that Allah has given you.
- Avoid actions and behaviours that lead to moral corruption and instead focus on righteousness.
- Regularly seek guidance from Allah and align your actions with His will.

Revealed in	Juz	Surah No.	No. of verses
Makkah	30	96	19

سُورَةُ العَلَق

SURAH AL-‘ALAQ

(THE CLOT)

عَلَّمَ ٱلْإِنسَٰنَ مَا لَمْ يَعْلَمْ ۝ كَلَّآ إِنَّ ٱلْإِنسَٰنَ لَيَطْغَىٰٓ ۝ أَن رَّءَاهُ ٱسْتَغْنَىٰٓ ۝ إِنَّ إِلَىٰ رَبِّكَ ٱلرُّجْعَىٰٓ ۝

“Taught humanity what they knew not. Most certainly, one exceeds all bounds once they think they are self-sufficient. ˹But˺ surely to your Lord is the return ˹of all˺.” (96:5-8)

Context

Surah Al-Alaq is the first revelation sent to Prophet Muhammad ﷺ through Angel Jibril (AS) in the Cave of Hira, near Makkah. The Surah encourages knowledge, reflection, and the recognition of Allah’s creation. It emphasises human beings’ dependence on Allah, as well as the significance of education and seeking knowledge

Topics

- The Beginning of Revelation
- Human Creation From a Clot of Blood
- Encouragement of Seeking Knowledge
- The Arrogance of the Disbeliever.
- The Responsibility to Obey Allah's Guidance.

Theme

Surah Al-Alaq highlights the importance of knowledge & the process of creation. It begins with a powerful call to read & seek knowledge, stressing that human beings are created from a simple clot of blood. It reflects on the origin of humanity & the greatness of Allah, urging believers to understand the depth of creation and the importance of humility and learning.

Virtues & Benefits

This Surah is the first revelation, making it a key Surah for understanding the start of Prophethood. Reciting this Surah can inspire the pursuit of knowledge & remind us of Allah’s creative power.

Ayah 1-5

Command to Read & Knowledge

These verses mark the first revelation given to the Prophet Muhammad ﷺ, emphasizing the importance of knowledge and divine wisdom. The command “Read” signifies the beginning of a new era of enlightenment, with God as the source of all learning. The mention of man being created “from a clot” highlights human fragility and dependence on the Creator. The reference to the pen and learning underscores the value of knowledge as a divine gift, enabling humanity to grow beyond its natural limitations.

Ayah 6-8

Human Arrogance

Despite receiving divine knowledge, humans often become arrogant. These verses warn against the tendency of individuals to overstep limits and act as if they are independent of Allah. When a person feels powerful or self-sufficient, they may reject divine guidance, thinking they no longer need it. However, the reminder “to your Lord is the return” serves as a warning that no matter how powerful someone feels, ultimate accountability lies with Allah.

Ayah 9-10

Oppression of Worshippers

These verses shift focus to an individual who attempts to prevent others from praying and worshiping Allah. This could refer to a historical figure opposing the early Muslims or represent anyone who suppresses faith and religious practice. The act of preventing prayer symbolizes opposition to truth and righteousness, as prayer is a direct connection between humans and their Creator.

Ayah 11-14

Righteousness vs. Rejection

A rhetorical question is posed: is the one preventing prayer truly on the path of guidance or advocating righteousness? The answer is clear—he has turned away from the truth. The verse “Does he not know that God sees?” serves as a powerful reminder that all actions, whether good or evil, are known to Allah, and no one can escape divine justice. This reinforces the idea of ultimate accountability.

Ayah 15-18

Consequences of Arrogance

A severe warning is issued against the one who persists in arrogance. The imagery of being “dragged by the forelock” conveys humiliation and divine punishment for those who deceive and commit sins. The verse “Let him call on his gang” sarcastically challenges the arrogant individual to summon his supporters, only for Allah to respond that He will call upon the angelic guards—representing divine justice and power over any human forces.

Ayah 19

Perseverance in Worship

The passage ends with a direct instruction: “No, do not obey him; but kneel down, and come near.” This is both a command and a reassurance. Believers are told not to submit to those who oppose their faith. Instead, they should remain steadfast in prayer, as prostration brings them closer to Allah. This verse highlights the ultimate source of strength—submission to Allah, rather than fear of worldly powers.

Lessons to Learn

- Knowledge is a vital part of the faith and comes directly from Allah. Seek knowledge with humility and sincerity.
- The process of human creation serves as a reminder of our humble beginnings and dependence on Allah for every blessing.
- Pride & arrogance lead to a rejection of the truth & will have consequences. Humility & submission to Allah’s will are crucial.

Action Steps

- Seek knowledge in all aspects of life, and approach learning with humility and a sense of gratitude to Allah.
- Remain mindful of your humble origins and avoid arrogance, recognising your dependence on Allah.
- Make an effort to reflect on Allah’s signs in the world around you and strive to strengthen your connection with Him.

Revealed in	Juz	Surah No.	No. of verses
Makkah	30	97	5

سُورَةُ القَدْر
SURAH AL-QADR
(THE POWER)

إِنَّآ أَنزَلْنَٰهُ فِى لَيْلَةِ ٱلْقَدْرِ ۝ وَمَآ أَدْرَىٰكَ مَا لَيْلَةُ ٱلْقَدْرِ ۝ لَيْلَةُ ٱلْقَدْرِ خَيْرٌ مِّنْ أَلْفِ شَهْرٍ ۝

"Indeed, 'it is' We 'Who' sent this 'Quran' down on the Night of Glory. And what will make you realize what the Night of Glory is? he Night of Glory is better than a thousand months." (97:1-3)

Context
Surah Al-Qadr was revealed to highlight the significance of Laylat al-Qadr (the Night of Decree), a night in the month of Ramadan that is better than a thousand months. The Surah emphasises the immense value and blessings of this night, where the Qur'an was first revealed, and the importance of worshipping Allah during this sacred time.

Topics
- The Greatness of Laylat al-Qadr.
- The Significance of the Quran's Revelation During This Night.
- The Night is Better Than a Thousand Months.
- Peace and blessings that descend on this night.

Theme
Surah Al-Qadr emphasises the greatness of the Night of Qadr (Laylat al-Qadr), a night of immense blessings, where angels descend to carry out Allah's commands. It highlights the importance of this night, which is better than a thousand months, & the significance of the Qur'an's revelation. The Surah also serves as a reminder of Allah's power and mercy in determining the fate of His creation.

Virtues & Benefits
This Surah holds great spiritual significance, as the blessings of Laylat al-Qadr is better than a thousand months. It is recommended to recite this Surah during the last ten nights of Ramadan.

Ayah 1
Revelation of Divine Guidance

This verse establishes the immense significance of the Night of Decree as the night when divine revelation was sent down. It is widely understood as the night in which the first verses of the Quran were revealed to the Prophet Muhammad ﷺ. This moment marks the beginning of God's final guidance to humanity, signifying a turning point in history. The emphasis on "We sent it down" highlights that this revelation is not from any human source but directly from the Creator, reinforcing its divine authority and wisdom.

Ayah 2
The Greatness of the Night

Here, the verse asks a rhetorical question: "But what will convey to you what the Night of Decree is?" This question serves to highlight the extraordinary and incomprehensible nature of this night. It suggests that the true depth of its importance goes beyond human understanding. By posing this question, the verse encourages deep contemplation, making it clear that this night is unlike any other, filled with divine blessings and significance that cannot be fully grasped by the human mind.

Ayah 3
A Night Worth More Than a Lifetime

The verse provides an astonishing statement: "The Night of Decree is better than a thousand months." This means that the worship, prayers, and good deeds performed on this single night are more valuable than those performed over the course of 83 years. This immense multiplication of rewards demonstrates God's infinite mercy and generosity, offering believers a once-a-year opportunity to achieve unparalleled spiritual growth. It signifies that one night of sincere devotion can have a greater impact than a lifetime of ordinary worship, making it a night of immense spiritual potential.

Ayah 4
Descent of Angels & Divine Decrees

This verse describes how the Night of Decree is not only a night of worship but also one of divine activity. It states that angels, along with the Spirit (commonly understood as Angel Gabriel), descend with divine decrees and instructions from God. This descent symbolises a sacred connection between the heavens and the earth, as angels spread peace, mercy, and blessings throughout the world. It is believed that on this night, destinies for the coming year—such as provisions, life spans, and significant events—are decreed. The presence of the angels signifies God's immense love and care for His creation, as they bring divine mercy to those who seek it.

Ayah 5
Essence of Peace & Tranquillity

The verse describes the Night of Decree as "Peace it is", indicating that this night is filled with divine tranquillity, free from evil, mischief, or harm. It is a night in which sincere worshippers are granted peace of heart, mind, and soul. Many scholars believe that on this night, Satan's influence is minimised, and the world is flooded with divine grace. This reinforces the idea that those who sincerely turn to God in worship, repentance, and supplication will find themselves enveloped in an unparalleled spiritual serenity.

Ayah 5
Timelessness of the Night's Blessings

The verse concludes by stating that this peace lasts "until the rise of dawn." This means that from sunset to the break of dawn, this night remains spiritually charged with divine blessings. It reassures believers that they have the entire night to engage in acts of worship, seek forgiveness, and make heartfelt supplications. The fact that this peace extends until dawn signifies that God's mercy is available throughout the night, giving worshippers every opportunity to attain divine rewards before a new day begins. This ending serves as a reminder that time is limited, and one should not waste the opportunity to benefit from the countless blessings of this sacred night.

Lessons to Learn
- The Night of Qadr is a time for deep reflection, worship, and seeking Allah's forgiveness.
- Allah's mercy is abundant, especially during Laylat al-Qadr, and believers should take full advantage of this sacred time.
- The presence of angels during this night symbolises peace, tranquillity, and Allah's blessings.

Action Steps
- In the last 10 nights of Ramadan, dedicate yourself to worship, prayer, and supplication, seeking the blessings of Laylat al-Qadr.
- Increase your recitation of the Qur'an, particularly during the blessed nights of Ramadan, to reflect on its guidance.
- Engage in sincere acts of worship, asking for forgiveness and mercy from Allah, particularly on Laylat al-Qadr.

Revealed in	Juz	Surah No.	No. of verses
Madina	30	98	8

سُورَةُ البَيِّنَةِ

SURAH AL-BAYYINAH

(THE CLEAR PROOF)

وَمَآ أُمِرُوٓا۟ إِلَّا لِيَعْبُدُوا۟ ٱللَّهَ مُخْلِصِينَ لَهُ ٱلدِّينَ حُنَفَآءَ وَيُقِيمُوا۟ ٱلصَّلَوٰةَ وَيُؤْتُوا۟ ٱلزَّكَوٰةَ

وَذَٰلِكَ دِينُ ٱلْقَيِّمَةِ ۝

"Even though they were only commanded to worship Allah 'alone' with sincere devotion to Him in all uprightness, establish prayer, and pay alms-tax. That is the upright Way." (98:5)

Context

Surah Al-Bayyina was revealed in response to the disbelievers' demand for clear signs from Allah. It emphasises the finality of the Prophet Muhammad's ﷺ mission, showing that his message is the final proof for humanity. The Surah addresses both the Jews and Christians who were waiting for the final messenger ﷺ and highlights that the clear evidence has arrived in the form of the Prophet ﷺ and the Qur'an.

Topics

- Clear Evidence of the Truth of Islam
- The Difference Between the Believers and Disbelievers
- The Rejection of the Message
- Reward for those who Act Righteous
- Ultimate Fate of disbelievers & the believers.

Theme

Surah Al-Bayyina focuses on the clear proof of Allah's final revelation, which has been manifested through the Prophet Muhammad ﷺ and the Qur'an. It emphasises that those who truly believe in Allah and follow the guidance brought by the Prophet ﷺ will be successful. The Surah also makes it clear that the previous communities who rejected the final message will face punishment.

Virtues & Benefits

Surah Al-Bayyina encourages following the guidance of the Prophet Muhammad ﷺ, which is the ultimate proof for humanity. It stresses the importance of believing in the final revelation.

Ayah 1 — The Arrival of Clear Evidence

This verse addresses two groups: the disbelievers among the People of the Scripture (Jews and Christians) and the polytheists. It states that they remained in their state of disbelief until a clear proof was presented to them. This suggests that divine guidance had always been available, but they only fully recognised their division after the arrival of the ultimate truth.

Ayah 2-3 — The Messenger & Purified Scriptures

These verses describe the "Clear Evidence" as a messenger from God who brings pure, non corrupted scriptures. The revelation he carries is filled with valuable guidance and wisdom, free from human distortion. This highlights the importance of divine revelation as a means of clarifying truth and guiding humanity toward righteousness.

Ayah 4 — Division Despite the Truth

Ironically, instead of uniting upon receiving divine guidance, previous communities divided further. This verse points out how people have historically rejected or misinterpreted revelation, leading to sectarianism and conflict. It serves as a warning against ignoring or distorting the truth once it has been made clear.

Ayah 5 — Core Commandments of Religion

Despite human divisions, the essence of true religion remains simple and unchanged: worshipping God sincerely, maintaining prayer, and giving to those in need. This verse emphasises that faith is not about complex doctrines but about devotion, discipline, and social responsibility—values that form the foundation of upright living.

Ayah 6 — The Fate of Disbelievers

This verse presents the consequences of rejecting the truth. Those who deny divine guidance, despite having access to it, are warned of eternal suffering. The phrase "worst of creatures" signifies that disbelief is not just a passive state but a condition that leads to spiritual and moral decay.

Ayah 7-8 — The Reward of the Righteous

The passage concludes with a contrast between the fate of disbelievers & believers. Those who have faith & live righteously are described as the best of creatures, destined for eternal bliss in paradise. Their ultimate reward is not just material comfort but divine pleasure—God's approval & their own fulfilment in His presence. This verse reassures believers that sincerity & righteousness lead to eternal peace and contentment.

Lessons to Learn

The Surah teaches the importance of recognising the final proof sent by Allah in the form of the Prophet Muhammad ﷺ & the Qur'an.

It highlights the distinction between true faith and stubborn rejection, which can lead to punishment.

Believers are encouraged to be patient, follow the truth, and trust that Allah's guidance is the final and complete path.

Action Steps

Strengthen your belief in the final message of Islam, & make it a point to reflect on the Qur'an & the life of the Prophet Muhammad ﷺ.

Strive to live according to the teachings of Islam, ensuring that both faith and actions are in line with the guidance provided by Allah.

When encountering resistance or rejection from others, remain steadfast in your faith and trust that the truth will prevail in the end.

Revealed in	Juz	Surah No.	No. of verses
Makkah	30	99	8

سُورَةُ الزَّلْزَلَةِ

SURAH AZ-ZALZALAH

(THE EARTHQUAKE)

فَمَن يَعْمَلْ مِثْقَالَ ذَرَّةٍ خَيْرًا يَرَهُ ۝ وَمَن يَعْمَلْ مِثْقَالَ ذَرَّةٍ شَرًّا يَرَهُ ۝

"So whoever does an atom's weight of good will see it. And whoever does an atom's weight of evil will see it." (99:7-8)

Context

Surah Az-Zalzalah was revealed to highlight the great events of the Day of Judgement when the earth will shake, and every person will be shown the results of their actions. It serves as a reminder of the ultimate accountability in front of Allah. It was revealed in response to people who were heedless of their deeds and the consequences of the hereafter.

Topics

- The Great Earthquake of the Day of Judgement.
- Revealing of All Deeds, Good & Bad.
- Accountability for Actions on the Day of Judgement.
- The Finality of Divine Justice.

Theme

The Surah focuses on the great earthquake that will take place on the Day of Judgement, followed by the earth revealing the deeds of its inhabitants. Every soul will be judged for its actions, whether good or bad. It serves as a reminder that human actions will be fully accounted for, and no one will escape the consequences.

Virtues & Benefits

Surah Az-Zalzalah is a reminder of the reality of the Day of Judgement & the accountability for one's actions. It brings awareness of the consequences of one's actions, motivating a righteous life.

Ayah 1

The Great Earthquake

This verse describes a powerful, earth-shattering event that signals the end of the world. The intensity of the earthquake is unlike anything witnessed before, symbolising the final upheaval before divine judgement. It serves as a reminder of the temporary nature of this world and the inevitable reality of resurrection and accountability.

Ayah 2

The Earth Revealing Its Burdens

Following the earthquake, the earth will release everything hidden within it. This can refer to the dead being resurrected from their graves or the earth revealing the secrets and deeds of humanity. It signifies the unveiling of all things, preparing for the final judgement where nothing remains concealed.

Ayah 3

Humanity's Shock & Confusion

People will be in utter shock and disbelief as they witness the extraordinary events unfolding before them. The ground they once walked on so confidently will be trembling and exposing its hidden truths. This verse highlights human vulnerability and the realisation that the worldly life they depended on is now coming to an end.

Ayah 4-5

The Earth's Testimony

On the Day of Judgement, the earth itself will speak, bearing witness to all the deeds performed upon it. Every action—good or bad—will be recorded and revealed. This shows that even inanimate creation is under divine command, and nothing escapes God's knowledge. The idea of the earth "telling its tales" reinforces the certainty of accountability.

Ayah 6

The Gathering for Judgment

Resurrected from their graves, people will gather in large crowds, awaiting their judgement. Every individual will be presented with the record of their actions, leaving no room for denial or excuses. This verse highlights the fairness of divine justice—each person will see exactly what they have done.

Ayah 7-8

The Ultimate Justice

The passage concludes with a powerful statement of divine justice: no deed, however small, will be overlooked. Even the tiniest act of kindness or wrongdoing will be accounted for. This serves as both a warning and a source of hope—every good deed matters, and no injustice will go unaddressed. It emphasises personal responsibility and the need to be mindful of one's actions in this world.

Lessons to Learn

Every individual's actions are recorded, and they will be judged accordingly.

There will be no escape from the consequences of our actions; the Day of Judgement is inevitable.

The earth will bear witness to what we have done, emphasising the complete transparency of the divine judgement process.

Action Steps

Regularly assess your actions, ensuring they align with the values of Islam and seek to live a righteous life.

Be mindful of the Day of Judgement and the accountability each person will face, reminding yourself of the ultimate consequences.

Engage in good deeds, charity, and acts of kindness, as these will be beneficial on the Day of Judgement.

Revealed in	Juz	Surah No.	No. of verses
Makkah	30	100	11

سُورَةُ العَادِيَاتِ

SURAH AL-ADIYAT

(THE COURSER)

إِنَّ رَبَّهُم بِهِمْ يَوْمَئِذٍ لَّخَبِيرٌ

"Surely their Lord is All-Aware of them on that Day." (100:11)

Context

This Surah was revealed in Makkah and addresses the ingratitude and heedlessness of human beings towards Allah, despite the blessings He has bestowed upon them. It uses the image of warhorses charging to describe how people are unaware of their ultimate accountability and how their ingratitude leads to their downfall.

Topics

- Imagery of Galloping Warhorses.
- Human Ingratitude Despite Receiving Blessings.
- The Intense Love for Wealth.
- Reality of Resurrection
- The Exposure of Hidden Secrets

Theme

The Surah emphasizes the ingratitude of humans towards their Creator despite the many blessings He provides. It uses the metaphor of fast-moving warhorses to illustrate human restlessness and their focus on worldly pursuits, forgetting their inevitable return to Allah. The Surah encourages mindfulness of one's actions and the coming Day of Judgment.

Virtues & Benefits

This Surah is a reminder of the impermanence of worldly matters & the importance of reflecting on one's actions. It brings awareness of human nature, reminding believers to stay humble.

Ayah 1-2

The Charge of the Racers

These verses paint a vivid picture of swift, determined horses galloping with full force, their breath heavy with exertion. The striking of their hooves against the ground creates sparks, symbolising power, urgency, and action. This imagery sets the stage for a deeper message, illustrating the intensity of worldly pursuits and how people charge forward in their ambitions, often without reflection on their ultimate purpose.

Ayah 3-5

The Sudden Attack

The scene continues with a surprise attack at dawn, a time when enemies are least prepared. The charging force raises dust, showing the chaos and intensity of the raid as they storm into the heart of battle. Metaphorically, this represents human beings rushing into worldly affairs with passion and recklessness, often unaware of the greater reality beyond their immediate struggles.

Ayah 6

Human Ingratitude

This verse shifts the focus from external action to internal reflection. It points out a fundamental flaw in human nature—ingratitude toward God. Despite being blessed with countless provisions and opportunities, people often fail to acknowledge the source of their blessings, taking them for granted. This ingratitude reflects a deeper spiritual negligence.

Ayah 7-8

Acknowledgment of Greed

Here, the verse suggests that humans, deep down, recognize their own flaws. They know of their ingratitude and attachment to material wealth, yet they persist in it. The phrase "fierce in his love of wealth" highlights the intensity of this attachment, showing that people prioritize material gain over spiritual fulfillment, often at the cost of morality and gratitude.

Ayah 9-10

The Revelation of Hidden Truths

A stark reminder of the afterlife, these verses highlight the moment when all secrets will be unveiled. The graves will give up their dead, and every hidden thought, feeling, and intention will be exposed. This serves as a warning: nothing remains concealed forever. Every action and intention will be accounted for, urging people to live with consciousness and sincerity.

Ayah 11

Divine Judgement & Complete Knowledge

The passage concludes with the ultimate reality—God's complete awareness and judgement. While people may deceive themselves or others in this world, nothing will be hidden from God. Every action, every thought, and every motive will be fully known. This verse serves as a final reminder to live with sincerity, gratitude, and awareness of the inevitable accountability before the Creator.

Lessons to Learn

Humans are often distracted by worldly pursuits, but they must remain aware of their accountability to Allah.

Ingratitude and heedlessness are dangerous, as they can lead to eventual regret on the Day of Judgment.

True success lies in being conscious of Allah and mindful of the Hereafter.

Action Steps

Reflect daily on your actions, and ensure they align with Allah's guidance, remembering that nothing escapes His knowledge.

Strive to maintain gratitude in your life by recognising and appreciating Allah's countless blessings.

Avoid excessive attachment to material possessions and focus on fulfilling your purpose of worshipping Allah.

Revealed in	Juz	Surah No.	No. of verses
Makkah	30	101	11

سُورَةُ القَارِعَةِ

SURAH AL-QARI'AH

(THE CALAMITY)

فَأَمَّا مَن ثَقُلَتْ مَوَٰزِينُهُۥ ۝ فَهُوَ فِى عِيشَةٍ رَّاضِيَةٍ ۝

"So as for those whose scale is heavy 'with good deeds', they will be in a life of bliss." (101:6-7)

Context

This Surah was revealed in Makkah, and it addresses the certainty of the Day of Judgment. It uses vivid and striking imagery to describe the calamity that will befall humanity when the world ends. The Surah calls attention to the gravity of that day, where people will be weighed based on their deeds.

Topics

- The Day of Judgment's Cataclysm
- Hearts Trembling in Fear
- Weighing of Deeds & Final Judgment
- Actions Determine Fate
- Contrast: Righteous vs. Wrongdoers

Theme

The central theme of Surah Al-Qari'ah is the Day of Judgment, where the world will be struck by a great calamity. On this day, the hearts of people will tremble, and the deeds of everyone will be weighed. The Surah stresses the importance of being aware of the accountability on that day and the consequences of one's actions.

Virtues & Benefits

This Surah serves as a powerful reminder of the finality of the Day of Judgement. Reciting this Surah regularly can strengthen one's awareness of accountability in the Hereafter.

Ayah 1-3

The Striking Calamity

The Surah opens by describing the overwhelming calamity, the "Qari'ah," that will strike the earth on the Day of Judgment. The use of strong, impactful imagery portrays the catastrophe as something that will shake everything to its core. The Surah warns of a time when nothing will be able to withstand the power of this event.

Ayah 4-5

The Impact of the Day

These verses describe the chaos that will unfold when the calamity strikes. The earth will be shaken violently, and people will be scattered like moths. The day will bring fear and trembling, as the outcome of each person's life will be determined based on their deeds. It emphasizes the unpredictable nature of the event.

Ayah 6

The Reckoning

The Surah transitions to the weighing of deeds, where each person's actions will be measured. Those whose deeds are heavy with good will receive a favorable outcome, while those whose deeds are light will face the consequences of their wrongdoings. This verse highlights the fairness of divine judgment.

Ayah 7

The Outcome for the Righteous

The Surah assures that those who have led righteous lives, with good deeds and faith, will experience salvation. Their balance of good deeds will save them from the fear and torment of the Day of Judgment. They will be rewarded for their efforts in this life, highlighting the importance of righteousness and piety.

Ayah 8

The Outcome for the Wicked

In contrast to the righteous, the Surah warns about the fate of those whose deeds are light and filled with wrongdoing. They will suffer greatly on that day, facing severe consequences for their actions. This section serves as a dire warning to those who are heedless of their responsibilities and actions in this world.

Ayah 9-11

The Final Division

The Surah concludes by contrasting the fates of the righteous & the wrongdoers. The righteous will be in a state of peace, while the wrongdoers will face punishment. These verses emphasise that the Day of Judgement will not be an ordinary event; it will determine eternal destinies, with the balance of one's deeds being the deciding factor.

Lessons to Learn

The Day of Judgment is certain, and everyone will be judged according to their deeds.

The Surah teaches the importance of working towards good deeds and faith, as they are the key to salvation.

Life is a test, and every individual's deeds will determine their eternal outcome.

Action Steps

Reflect daily on your actions and strive to live in a way that aligns with the teachings of Islam.

Make an effort to perform good deeds, especially those that are sincere and beneficial for others.

Strengthen your relationship with Allah through regular worship, prayer, and remembrance.

Revealed in	Juz	Surah No.	No. of verses
Makkah	30	102	8

سُورَةُ التَّكَاثُرِ

SURAH AT-TAKATHUR

(THE RIVALRY IN WORLD INCREASE)

ثُمَّ لَتُسْـَٔلُنَّ يَوْمَئِذٍ عَنِ ٱلنَّعِيمِ

"Then, on that Day, you will definitely be questioned about 'your worldly' pleasures." (102:8)

Context

This Surah was revealed as a warning to those consumed by worldly competition. The people of Makkah were obsessed with wealth, status, and power, distracting them from the remembrance of Allah. This Surah reminds them that such pursuits are temporary and that they will soon face the reality of the Hereafter.

Topics

- Distraction of Worldly Competition
- Inevitable Reality of Death
- Certainty of Facing the Hereafter
- Consequences of Ignoring the Truth
- Importance of Recognising Life's True Purpose

Theme

The central theme of Surah At-Takathur is the destructive nature of materialism and the consequences of being overly attached to worldly possessions. It warns that people will regret their obsession with wealth and power when they face death and the Hereafter. The Surah urges reflection on life's true purpose and preparation for the final accountability before Allah.

Virtues & Benefits

A reminder of life's true purpose and the deception of material wealth. Encourages gratitude for Allah's blessings. A powerful wake-up call to prepare for the Hereafter.

Ayah 1-2

Materialistic Distraction

People remain distracted by their pursuit of wealth, power, and worldly achievements, competing with one another for more possessions and influence. They become so engrossed in this race that they forget their true purpose in life. This unhealthy obsession keeps them away from seeking Allah's guidance and preparing for the Hereafter.

Ayah 2

Death Ends World Delusions

This race for material gain continues until death arrives. No matter how much a person accumulates, they will eventually be placed in a grave, leaving everything behind. At that moment, the reality of their deeds and priorities will become clear.

Ayah 3-4

Reality of the Hereafter

The Surah warns that if only people had true knowledge, they would not be so obsessed with the temporary pleasures of this world. They would realize that their wealth and status hold no value in the Hereafter, where only faith and righteous deeds matter

Ayah 5-6

Inevitable Hellfire

A warning is given that everyone will be shown the Hellfire with absolute certainty. The veil of deception will be lifted, and people will see the consequences of their heedlessness. This moment will be filled with regret for those who ignored the truth.

Ayah 7

Certainty of Judgment

Not only will people see Hellfire, but they will also experience it firsthand if they failed to prepare for the Hereafter. The punishment will be undeniable, proving that the warnings in this life were true.

Ayah 8

Accountability for Blessings

Finally, the Surah ends with a powerful statement: Every individual will be questioned about the blessings they enjoyed. This includes wealth, health, time, and opportunities given by Allah. Did they use these for righteous purposes, or were they wasted in worldly distractions?

Lessons to Learn

Wealth and status are temporary; the Hereafter is eternal.

Being consumed by material gain leads to regret.

Every blessing will be accounted for on the Day of Judgment.

True success lies in preparing for the Afterlife, not accumulating wealth.

Action Steps

Reflect on whether worldly pursuits are distracting you from worship.

Express gratitude by using wealth and blessings for good.

Prioritise spiritual growth over material success.

Remind yourself daily that life is temporary, & the Hereafter is permanent.

سُورَةُ العَصْرِ

SURAH AL-'ASR

(THE DECLINING DAY)

Revealed in	Juz	Surah No.	No. of verses
Makkah	30	103	3

وَٱلْعَصْرِ ۝ إِنَّ ٱلْإِنسَـٰنَ لَفِى خُسْرٍ ۝ إِلَّا ٱلَّذِينَ ءَامَنُوا۟ وَعَمِلُوا۟ ٱلصَّـٰلِحَـٰتِ وَتَوَاصَوْا۟
بِٱلْحَقِّ وَتَوَاصَوْا۟ بِٱلصَّبْرِ ۝

"By the 'passage of' time! Surely humanity is in 'grave' loss, except those who have faith, do good, and urge each other to the truth, and urge each other to perseverance." (103:1-3)

Context

This Surah serves as a concise yet powerful reminder of the fleeting nature of time and the four essential qualities needed to attain success in this world and the Hereafter. It warns against wasting life in heedlessness and emphasizes the importance of faith, good deeds, truth, and patience as the path to salvation.

Topics

- Importance of Time
- Inevitable Loss of Those Who Waste Time
- Four Qualities of Successful People
- Faith & Good Deeds are Essential For Salvation
- The Importance of Truth and Patience

Theme

Surah Al-Asr encapsulates the essence of success and failure in just three verses. It declares that all of humanity is at a loss, except those who embody four key traits: faith, righteous deeds, advising one another to truth, and encouraging patience. This Surah highlights the value of time and the urgency of using it wisely before it runs out.

Virtues & Benefits

Teaches the four essential qualities for salvation. Encourages time management, faith, good deeds, and patience. Helps believers stay motivated in their spiritual journey.

Ayah 1

The Oath by Time

The Surah begins with Allah swearing by "Asr" (time or the declining day) to emphasize its significance and fleeting nature. Time is one of the greatest blessings, yet it is constantly slipping away. This verse urges us to reflect on how we use our time, as every moment that passes is one we can never get back.

Ayah 2

Humanity is at a Loss

Allah declares that all of humanity is doomed to failure, except those who embrace a righteous path. This loss is not just in worldly terms but also in the spiritual and eternal sense. The verse serves as a stark reminder that without faith and good actions, time will pass in vain, leading to ultimate regret.

Ayah 3

Faith Leads to Success

The first condition for salvation is faith (Iman). A strong belief in Allah, the Hereafter, and divine guidance gives meaning to life and shapes a person's actions. Without faith, people wander aimlessly, wasting their time and potential. This verse highlights that faith is the foundation of success.

Ayah 1-3

Good Deeds Define Faith

Faith alone is not enough; it must be followed by righteous actions. Good deeds include acts of worship, kindness, charity, and justice. This verse teaches that success requires actively living out one's faith, as true belief manifests through good conduct.

Ayah 1-3

Truth Requires Unity

Truth (Haqq) refers to believing in and spreading what is right, upholding justice, and following divine guidance. This verse emphasizes that success is not individualistic; believers must help and remind others to stay on the right path. The pursuit of truth is a communal responsibility.

Ayah 1-3

Patience Builds Strength

Patience (Sabr) is essential for enduring life's challenges, maintaining faith, and persevering in good deeds. Hardships and struggles are inevitable, but true believers support one another in staying steadfast. This verse teaches that spiritual success requires resilience and collective encouragement.

Lessons to Learn

Time is valuable use it wisely.

Faith and righteous actions must go together.

Helping others and spreading truth strengthens society.

Patience is necessary to overcome difficulties.

Success is not in wealth or status, but in faith and character.

Action Steps

Reflect on how you spend your time and set meaningful goals.

Strengthen your faith through worship, prayer, and seeking knowledge.

Recite and internalise this Surah to remind yourself of life's true purpose.

Revealed in	Juz	Surah No.	No. of verses
Makkah	30	104	9

سُورَةُ الهُمَزَةِ

SURAH AL-HUMAZAH

(THE SLANDERER)

وَيْلٌ لِّكُلِّ هُمَزَةٍ لُّمَزَةٍ ۞ ٱلَّذِى جَمَعَ مَالًا وَعَدَّدَهُۥ ۞ يَحْسَبُ أَنَّ مَالَهُۥٓ أَخْلَدَهُۥ ۞

"Woe to every backbiter, slander, who amasses wealth 'greedily' and counts it 'repeatedly', thinking that their wealth will make them immortal!" (104:1-3)

Context

This Surah was revealed to condemn the arrogance and greed of the wealthy elite in Makkah, who mocked others and hoarded wealth. It serves as a warning to those who slander, gossip, and put their trust in material possessions, thinking wealth grants them eternal security.

Topics

- Condemnation of Those Who Slander
- Arrogance & Pride Associated With Wealth & Status
- Consequences of Engaging in Harmful Behaviour
- Inevitable Punishment for Those Who Harm Others

Theme

The Surah highlights the destructive consequences of arrogance, backbiting, and greed. It warns those who mock and slander others, believing their wealth will protect them, that they will face severe punishment in the Hereafter. The Surah emphasizes that true success is not in wealth but in righteousness and good character.

Virtues & Benefits

This Surah serves as a reminder of the consequences of malicious behaviour, particularly backbiting & slander. It encourages self-reflection & mindfulness about the harm caused by words & actions.

Ayah 1 — Warning to Slanderers & Mockers

The Surah begins with a stern warning to those who habitually mock, ridicule, and belittle others. The word "Humazah" refers to someone who slanders in secret, while "Lumazah" refers to someone who insults openly. This verse teaches that verbal abuse, whether public or private, has severe consequences, as it leads to social corruption and injustice.

Ayah 2 — The Deception of Wealth

This verse criticizes those obsessed with accumulating wealth, believing it will bring them eternal security. Such people hoard wealth without using it for good, thinking their riches define their worth. The verse serves as a reminder that material possessions are temporary and that true success lies in generosity and righteousness.

Ayah 3 — False Sense of Security

Many believe that money grants power and protection, making them untouchable. However, wealth cannot stop death or prevent divine punishment. This verse exposes the delusional thinking of the arrogant and highlights that only faith and good deeds ensure true success.

Ayah 4-5 — The Reality of Al-Hutamah

The term "Al-Hutamah" refers to a crushing and consuming fire in Hell, a punishment reserved for those who mock and hoard wealth unjustly. The verse reminds us that no amount of wealth or status can protect one from divine justice.

Ayah 6-7 — The Intensity of Hellfire

Unlike ordinary fire, Hellfire will burn not just the body but also the heart, symbolizing the ultimate suffering. This description emphasizes that arrogance, mockery, and greed will lead to unbearable torment, as these sins corrupt the heart and soul.

Ayah 8-9 — Eternal Punishment

The Surah concludes by describing the inescapable nature of Hell, where the sinners will be locked in with no escape. The "columns" indicate a sealed, enclosed torment, showing that those who reject faith and misuse wealth will have no relief from their punishment.

Lessons to Learn

Arrogance & pride, especially based on wealth or status, are destructive traits that can lead to loss in both this life & the Hereafter.

Backbiting and slander not only harm others but also lead to severe consequences for the one who engages in such behaviour.

Wealth and status will not protect a person from the consequences of their actions, and humility is vital in seeking Allah's mercy.

Action Steps

Avoid engaging in slander, gossip, or negative speech about others. Be mindful of your words and their potential impact.

Focus on humility and gratitude, recognizing that wealth, power, or status are temporary and should not lead to pride.

Encourage others to speak kindly and avoid backbiting, promoting an environment of trust and respect.

Revealed in	Juz	Surah No.	No. of verses
Makkah	30	105	5

سُورَةُ الفِيلِ

SURAH AL-FIL

(THE ELEPHANT)

أَلَمْ تَرَ كَيْفَ فَعَلَ رَبُّكَ بِأَصْحَٰبِ ٱلْفِيلِ ۝ أَلَمْ يَجْعَلْ كَيْدَهُمْ فِى تَضْلِيلٍ ۝ وَأَرْسَلَ عَلَيْهِمْ طَيْرًا أَبَابِيلَ ۝

"Have you not seen 'O Prophet' how your Lord dealt with the Army of the Elephant? Did He not frustrate their scheme? For He sent against them flocks of birds" (105:1-3)

Context

The Surah was revealed in the context of the invasion of Makkah by the army of Abraha, who attempted to destroy the Kaabah using elephants. Allah sent birds carrying stones of clay to defeat the army. This miraculous event emphasized Allah's power and the protection of the sacred House of Allah.

Topics

- The Attack on the Kaaba
- Divine Protection
- Allah's Miraculous Intervention
- Humbling the Arrogant
- Victory Through Faith & Reliance on Allah

Theme

Surah Al-Fil emphasizes the divine intervention in protecting the Kaabah and Makkah from the invasion of Abraha's army. The Surah illustrates that no matter how powerful an enemy may be, Allah is always able to defend His sacred places and His believers. The defeat of the invaders serves as a powerful reminder of Allah's omnipotence and the futility of human arrogance in the face of His power.

Virtues & Benefits

It teaches that no matter how powerful someone or something may seem, Allah's power is ultimate. This Surah serves as a reminder of how Allah protected His sacred House and His believers.

Ayah 1

The Attack of Abraha's Army

This verse begins with a rhetorical question, drawing attention to the event when Abraha, the ruler of Yemen, marched with his army, including elephants, to destroy the Kaaba. Allah refers to the attackers as the "Owners of the Elephant" to highlight the significance of their invasion. Despite their strength and preparations, Allah is reminding the Quraysh of His protection over the Kaaba, showing that no one can harm what Allah wishes to preserve.

Ayah 2

The Failure of Their Plans

Despite the well-organized military campaign, Allah made their plans fail. This verse highlights the futility of human efforts when they are in opposition to Allah's will. The soldiers of Abraha had everything in their favor—powerful armies, war elephants, and strategic plans—but none of that mattered. Their mission to destroy the Kaaba ended in failure because Allah, in His infinite wisdom, thwarted their attempts.

Ayah 3

The Divine Intervention

As the army marched towards the Kaaba, Allah sent flocks of birds that rained stones of Sijjil (a fiery substance) upon them. This was a miraculous intervention from Allah, showing that even the most powerful armies cannot succeed without His permission. The verse reminds the believers of Allah's ultimate control over all things, and how He can intervene in ways that are beyond human understanding to protect His sacred places.

Ayah 4

The Punishment with Stones

The birds that Allah sent carried stones that struck the invading army, destroying them. The term Sijjil refers to the fiery stones that were specifically sent to punish the disbelievers. The verse emphasizes the divine retribution against those who attempted to challenge Allah's power. It serves as a lesson in how Allah's punishment can be swift and decisive, overwhelming even the strongest of forces.

Ayah 5

The Complete Destruction

The invaders, once mighty and proud, were reduced to a state of complete destruction, as if they were withered straw eaten by animals. This final verse underscores the total defeat of Abraha's army. Their arrogance and pride were shattered, and they were rendered powerless by Allah's will. It's a reminder that no matter how powerful a force may appear, if it opposes Allah, it will ultimately be humbled.

Ayah 1-5

Lesson of Divine Power

Surah Al-Fil is a powerful reminder of Allah's ability to defend His sacred places and control the universe. The defeat of Abraha's army by birds carrying stones symbolizes Allah's omnipotence and His supreme control over all things. It also highlights that humans should never challenge or underestimate the power of Allah. This Surah teaches us to place our trust in Allah and recognize that He is the ultimate source of protection, guidance, and strength.

Lessons to Learn

Trust in Allah's Protection: No matter what challenges you face, know that Allah has the power to protect and guide you.

Powerlessness of Arrogance: The story of Abraha teaches, that those who challenge Allah's will, will be humbled, despite their power.

Faith in Divine Will: The Surah reinforces that Allah's plan prevails over human efforts, and we must place our trust in Him.

Action Steps

Rely on Allah's Help: In facing difficulties, turn to Allah for support, knowing that He has power over all things.

Reflect on Divine Power: Take time to reflect on Allah's mercy and protection in your life, and be grateful for His continuous blessings.

Humility and Gratitude: Acknowledge that all power and success come from Allah, and remain humble in your achievements.

Revealed in	Juz	Surah No.	No. of verses
Makkah	30	106	4

سُورَةُ قُرَيْشٍ

SURAH QURAYSH

(THE QURAYSH)

فَلْيَعْبُدُوا۟ رَبَّ هَٰذَا ٱلْبَيْتِ ۝ ٱلَّذِىٓ أَطْعَمَهُم مِّن جُوعٍ وَءَامَنَهُم مِّنْ خَوْفٍۭ ۝

"let them worship the Lord of this 'Sacred' House, Who has fed them against hunger and made them secure against fear." (106:3-4)

Context

This Surah was revealed to remind the Quraysh tribe of Allah's mercy and blessings, especially the security and prosperity they enjoyed due to their trade routes. It calls on them to acknowledge Allah's favor and to worship Him sincerely in gratitude for His continuous blessings.

Topics

- Allah's Blessings on Quraysh
- Importance of Gratitude to Allah
- Allah's Provision of Peace and Prosperity
- Call to Worship Allah Alone

Theme

Surah Quraysh highlights the blessings and provisions Allah has given to the Quraysh tribe, including peace, prosperity, and safety in their trade journeys. It calls them to show gratitude and worship Allah alone, recognizing that these blessings are a result of His grace and protection.

Virtues & Benefits

Teaches the importance of gratitude for the blessings of Allah in our lives.
Reciting Surah Quraysh encourages mindfulness about the peace and security Allah has provided.

Ayah 1

Blessing of Security

The Surah begins by highlighting the security enjoyed by the Quraysh tribe in their trading journeys. They were granted peace and protection during their travels, both in winter and summer. This security wasn't accidental, but a divine blessing from Allah, who ensured their safety. It reminds the Quraysh of Allah's mercy, urging them to recognize the special favor they have received from the Creator.

Ayah 2

Gratitude for Prosperous Trade Routes

The Quraysh enjoyed prosperity from their trade routes in both the winter and summer seasons, enabling them to become a wealthy tribe. The verse emphasizes that these favorable trade conditions were not just coincidences but were orchestrated by Allah's will. The blessing of prosperity is a result of Allah's mercy, and this prosperity should be met with gratitude and worship of Allah, who made it all possible.

Ayah 3

Worshiping the Lord of the Kaabah

In response to the blessings of security and prosperity, Allah calls the Quraysh to worship the Lord of the Kaaba, the One who granted them these gifts. This is a direct command for the tribe to acknowledge that all blessings come from Allah and to dedicate their worship solely to Him. The verse serves as a reminder that true gratitude is shown through worship and submission to the Creator.

Ayah 4

Allah's Provision of Sustenance

This verse emphasizes Allah's nourishment and protection over the Quraysh. Allah provided for them during times of hunger and saved them from harm and fear. Their sustenance and security were safeguarded by Allah's mercy, showing the depth of His care for them. The verse underscores that these blessings are from Allah, and they should not be taken for granted but acknowledged with sincere worship.

Ayah 1-4

Call for Acknowledgement & Worship

The blessings described in this Surah are meant to lead the Quraysh to an acknowledgment of Allah's supreme power and mercy. By reminding the Quraysh of the protection they received during their trade routes and the food provided during times of need, the Surah calls for gratitude. The worship of Allah alone is not only a response to His blessings but also a means of continuing to receive His protection and provisions.

Ayah 1-4

Significance of Worship

The Surah concludes by directing the Quraysh to worship the Lord of the Kaabah, which represents the central place of worship for them. This reinforces the idea that gratitude for Allah's blessings isn't complete without worship. The Quraysh are urged to understand that their well-being is the result of Allah's mercy and that true worship should flow from this recognition. The Surah serves as a powerful reminder of how gratitude to Allah should shape the lives of the believers.

Lessons to Learn

Gratitude for Allah's blessings should lead to sincere worship.

Prosperity and peace are gifts from Allah, and we must acknowledge them.

The Kaabah is a symbol of Allah's mercy and protection for Makkah and its people.

Action Steps

Show gratitude by dedicating your worship solely to Allah.

Reflect on Allah's protection in daily life and give thanks for your safety.

Perform acts of worship with the intention of thanking Allah for His mercy.

Revealed in	Juz	Surah No.	No. of verses
Makkah	30	107	7

سُورَةُ المَاعُونِ

SURAH AL-MA'UN

(THE SMALL KINDNESS)

فَوَيْلٌ لِّلْمُصَلِّينَ ۝ ٱلَّذِينَ هُمْ عَن صَلَاتِهِمْ سَاهُونَ ۝ ٱلَّذِينَ هُمْ يُرَآءُونَ ۝ وَيَمْنَعُونَ ٱلْمَاعُونَ ۝

"So woe to those 'hypocrites' who pray yet are unmindful of their prayers; those who 'only' show off, and refuse to give 'even the simplest' aid." (107:4-7)

Context

This Surah was revealed in Makkah, and it primarily addresses those who outwardly perform acts of worship but neglect basic acts of kindness and social responsibility. The Surah was likely revealed to criticize hypocrites and remind people that true worship is not just ritual, but also involves caring for the less fortunate and fulfilling one's social obligations.

Topics

- Neglecting Small Kindness
- Faith and Social Responsibility
- Helping the Poor
- Rebuking Those Who Show Off Worship
- Worship Reflects in Actions

Theme

Surah Al-Ma'un emphasizes the importance of sincerity in worship and the connection between faith and social responsibility. It criticizes those who neglect basic acts of kindness, such as helping the poor, while performing outward acts of worship. The Surah calls for genuine care for others, highlighting the significance of fulfilling basic needs and showing kindness in daily life.

Virtues & Benefits

This Surah helps to foster empathy & a sense of duty toward those in need.
Reciting this Surah can instill humility, reminding individuals to avoid hypocrisy & focus on fulfilling the needs of others.

Ayah 1
Denying the Religion

This verse addresses the one who rejects faith and the moral responsibilities that come with it. In many religious and ethical traditions, belief is not just about acknowledging a higher power but also about acting justly. The passage highlights that disbelief is often linked to moral corruption, as rejecting divine guidance can lead to neglecting the rights of others.

Ayah 2
Mistreatment of Orphans

Orphans are among the most vulnerable in society, and mistreating them is a sign of a hardened heart. In many religious and ethical teachings, caring for orphans is a fundamental moral duty. This verse points out that a person who denies faith often lacks compassion, failing to care for those in need, particularly children who have no guardians.

Ayah 3
Neglecting the Poor

The verse criticizes those who do not encourage feeding the poor, emphasizing that faith should manifest in actions. True righteousness involves helping those who struggle to meet their basic needs. This verse implies that denying the importance of helping the less fortunate is an indication of moral failure.

Ayah 4
Warning to Those Who Pray

This verse might seem surprising at first, as prayer is generally seen as a righteous act. However, it serves as a warning against those who pray for show rather than out of sincerity. It suggests that ritual acts of worship are meaningless if they are not accompanied by genuine faith and good deeds.

Ayah 5
Heedlessness in Prayer

Being heedless of prayer means being careless about its timing, meaning, and purpose. It suggests a lack of sincerity in worship, where prayers become a mere routine rather than a sincere connection with Allah. This verse highlights that faith is not just about performing rituals but about embodying true devotion and awareness.

Ayah 6-7
Hypocrisy & Withholding Help

The passage concludes by condemning those who display outward piety but fail to help others. It criticizes hypocrisy—those who appear religious but withhold assistance from those in need. True faith, according to this teaching, is demonstrated through both devotion to Allah and service to humanity.

Lessons to Learn

True faith involves not only ritual worship but also caring for the needy and fulfilling social obligations.

Arrogance and pride undermine the essence of worship, and hypocritical behavior leads to spiritual failure.

Small acts of kindness are essential components of a sincere relationship with Allah.

Action Steps

Perform acts of kindness daily: help the poor, assist orphans, and provide aid when possible.

Be sincere in worship: focus on your prayers and acts of devotion with intention.

Avoid showing off: keep your acts of worship & good deeds private.

Revealed in	Juz	Surah No.	No. of verses
Makkah	30	108	3

سُورَةُ الكَوثَرِ

SURAH AL-KAWTHAR

(THE ABUNDANCE)

إِنَّآ أَعْطَيْنَـٰكَ ٱلْكَوْثَرَ ۝ فَصَلِّ لِرَبِّكَ وَٱنْحَرْ ۝ إِنَّ شَانِئَكَ هُوَ ٱلْأَبْتَرُ ۝

"Indeed, We have granted you 'O Prophet' abundant goodness. So pray and sacrifice to your Lord 'alone'. Only the one who hates you is truly cut off 'from any goodness'." (108:1-3)

Context

Surah Al-Kawthar was revealed in response to the grief of the Prophet Muhammad ﷺ who had lost his sons and faced severe opposition from his enemies. The disbelievers mocked him, saying he had no legacy. In this Surah, Allah comforted His Messenger ﷺ by promising him great reward, abundance, and a legacy greater than anything they could understand.

Topics

- Allah's Abundant Blessings to Prophet Muhammad ﷺ
- The Concept of Divine Generosity
- The Importance of Prayer and Sacrifice
- Encouragement of Gratitude to Allah

Theme

Surah Al-Kawthar speaks of Allah's immense blessings granted to the Prophet Muhammad ﷺ. The Surah highlights Allah's generosity and the unimaginable rewards He bestows on His beloved Prophet ﷺ. The Surah also emphasizes gratitude, worship, and devotion to Allah as the means to access these divine blessings, encouraging believers to give thanks through prayer and sacrifice.

Virtues & Benefits

A powerful reminder of Allah's abundant blessings and rewards.
It is said to offer blessings and abundance to those who recite it regularly.

Ayah 1

Allah's Promise of Abundance

This verse announces Allah's immense gift to the Prophet Muhammad ﷺ in the form of Al-Kawthar, a special blessing that encompasses abundant good. Al-Kawthar is often understood as a river in Paradise, representing endless blessings, but it can also symbolize Allah's grace in terms of guidance, legacy, and mercy.

Ayah 2

The Command for Gratitude

Following the immense blessing, the Surah instructs the Prophet ﷺ and believers to offer prayer (Salat) and sacrifice as acts of worship. This verse emphasizes that devotion to Allah is the way to show gratitude for His blessings. Prayer and sacrifice are means of maintaining a connection with the divine.

Ayah 3

Allah's Assurance

This verse reassures the Prophet Muhammad ﷺ that his enemies—the disbelievers who mocked him—would have no legacy. The true loss is theirs, as they are cut off from Allah's mercy and reward. This was a consolation to the Prophet ﷺ, reinforcing that his mission and legacy would remain eternal, while his enemies' efforts would be in vain.

Ayah 1-3

The Blessings of Al-Kawthar

The Surah highlights the greatness of Allah's blessings, which include not only the river of Kawthar in Paradise but also the Prophet's ﷺ legacy through Islam. It shows that Allah's mercy is greater than worldly losses or mockery. Al-Kawthar symbolizes all the good granted to the Prophet Muhammad ﷺ, including the growth of Islam, the blessing of guidance, and eternal rewards.

Ayah 1-3

A Call to Gratitude

The Surah emphasizes the importance of worship in showing gratitude for Allah's gifts. It teaches that prayer and sacrifice are not only acts of worship but also reminders of the abundant blessings one has received. Gratitude isn't just words, but actions that reflect true devotion to Allah.

Ayah 1-3

Reassurance for Believers

This Surah is also a source of comfort for all believers, reminding them that even in difficult times or moments of loss, Allah's blessings and mercy are far greater. It teaches that faith and gratitude lead to everlasting rewards, and those who remain devoted to Allah will find true success, while the enemies of faith will ultimately face defeat.

Lessons to Learn

Gratitude is key: acknowledge Allah's blessings through worship.

Allah's blessings are vast: never doubt the abundance of His mercy and generosity.

Enemies of faith will not succeed: trust that Allah will protect and bless His believers.

Action Steps

Seek Allah's mercy: remind yourself that His blessings are far greater than any trials.

Reflect on Allah's abundant gifts: whether material or spiritual, and express thanks through worship.

Trust in divine support: Allah's help is always with the faithful.

Revealed in	Juz	Surah No.	No. of verses
Makkah	30	109	6

سُورَةُ الكَافِرُونَ

SURAH AL-KAFIRUN

(THE DISBELIEVERS)

لَآ أَعْبُدُ مَا تَعْبُدُونَ ۝

"I do not worship what you worship," (109:2)

Context

Surah Al-Kafirun was revealed in response to the disbelievers' requests for the Prophet Muhammad ﷺ to compromise or merge aspects of Islam with their beliefs. The disbelievers sought a middle ground, proposing that the Prophet ﷺ worship their idols in exchange for some of their worshiping Allah. This Surah firmly rejects such compromise.

Topics

- The Rejection of Idol Worship.
- Islam vs. Disbelief
- Uncompromising Monotheism
- Prophet Muhammad's ﷺ Refusal
- Allegiance to Allah Alone

Theme

Surah Al-Kafirun emphasizes the complete separation between belief in Allah and disbelief. It rejects any attempt to blend or compromise between Islam and other belief systems. It highlights the resolute stance of the Prophet Muhammad ﷺ and the Muslim community, stressing that their worship is solely dedicated to Allah, with no room for polytheism or idolatry.

Virtues & Benefits

It is a reminder of the uncompromising nature of Islamic monotheism and helps reinforce the identity of Muslims.

It is a source of spiritual strength for those who face challenges to their faith.

Ayah 1
Rejection of Polytheism

The Surah begins with the declaration that the Prophet Muhammad ﷺ addresses the disbelievers, stating that he does not worship what they worship. This sets the tone for the absolute rejection of any form of idolatry or polytheism. It emphasizes that Islam is distinct from all other religions.

Ayah 2
Rejection of the Disbelievers'

The second verse is a direct challenge to the disbelievers, affirming that their worship is not shared by the Prophet Muhammad ﷺ and his followers. This reinforces the idea of complete separation in beliefs and practices. It emphasizes the exclusivity of worshiping Allah alone.

Ayah 3
The Disbelievers' Choice

The verse clarifies that the disbelievers have the freedom to continue their own worship, but the Prophet Muhammad ﷺ and the believers will not partake in their practices. This reflects respect for personal choice while reaffirming the non-negotiable nature of Islamic monotheism.

Ayah 4
Non-Compromise in Worship

The verse emphasizes that the Prophet ﷺ and the Muslims will never worship the gods of the disbelievers. This continues the message of absolute devotion to Allah alone and underscores the seriousness of adhering to the oneness of God. It rejects any attempt to dilute the message of Islam.

Ayah 5
Clear Declaration of Faith

The Surah states that the disbelievers have their own faith, and the Muslims have theirs. It makes a clear distinction between the two, reinforcing the concept of religious separation. It highlights the sovereignty of Allah and the commitment of Muslims to worship Him alone.

Ayah 6
Final Rejection of Polytheism

The final verse of the Surah is a firm and final rejection of any shared worship. The Prophet Muhammad ﷺ declares his loyalty to Allah and announces that he will not compromise his faith in any way. The Surah ends with a declaration of the complete separation between belief in Allah and disbelief.

Lessons to Learn

Muslims must distinguish themselves from disbelief and remain firm in their worship of Allah.

Every individual has the right to their own faith, but Muslims are called to stand firm in their own belief without succumbing to external pressures or attempts at compromise.

Action Steps

Regularly affirm your commitment to worshiping Allah alone, avoiding any form of shirk (polytheism).

Stand firm in your faith when faced with challenges or peer pressure that might compromise your beliefs.

Revealed in	Juz	Surah No.	No. of verses
Madinah	30	110	3

سُورَةُ النَّصۡرِ

SURAH AN-NASR

(THE DIVINE HELP)

إِذَا جَآءَ نَصۡرُ ٱللَّهِ وَٱلۡفَتۡحُ ۝ وَرَأَيۡتَ ٱلنَّاسَ يَدۡخُلُونَ فِي دِينِ ٱللَّهِ أَفۡوَاجٗا ۝ فَسَبِّحۡ بِحَمۡدِ رَبِّكَ وَٱسۡتَغۡفِرۡهُۚ إِنَّهُۥ كَانَ تَوَّابَۢا ۝

"When Allah's 'ultimate' help comes and the victory 'over Mecca is achieved', and you 'O Prophet' see the people embracing Allah's Way in crowds, then glorify the praises of your Lord and seek His forgiveness, for certainly He is ever Accepting of Repentance." (110:1-3)

Context

Surah An-Nasr was revealed towards the end of the Prophet Muhammad's ﷺ mission, following the conquest of Makkah. It marks the victory of Islam, signifying that the mission of the Prophet ﷺ was near its completion. The Surah was also a reminder that Allah's help and support had been granted to the Prophet ﷺ in his mission and that Islam was becoming dominant.

Topics

- Victory and Help From Allah
- Gratitude for Divine Success
- Significance of Repentance After Success
- The Final Victory of Islam

Theme

Surah An-Nasr emphasizes the victory and divine support that Allah granted to Prophet Muhammad ﷺ and the Muslim community. It serves as a reminder of the importance of gratitude, humility, and turning to Allah in moments of success. The Surah also highlights that after a victory or achievement, the believer should praise Allah and seek His forgiveness.

Virtues & Benefits

A reminder of Allah's support in times of victory.
This Surah expresses the completeness of the Prophet's ﷺ mission.

Ayah 1

The Divine Help and Victory

The Surah begins with the promise of victory from Allah, marking the conquest of Makkah. This was a pivotal moment for Islam, as the people of Makkah accepted Islam after years of hostility. The verse signifies the fulfilment of Allah's promise of helping the Prophet ﷺ and his followers triumph over their adversaries.

Ayah 2

People Entering Islam

This verse foretells that after Makkah's conquest, many people would accept Islam. The mass conversion was a sign of Allah's mercy and the spread of truth. It reflects the great success of the Prophet's ﷺ mission and Allah's divine help in bringing people to faith in great numbers.

Ayah 3

Seeking Forgiveness

After victory, the Surah instructs believers to praise and thank Allah for His divine help. It also highlights the importance of seeking forgiveness for any shortcomings, even after success, as Allah is the One who accepts repentance. This teaches that in moments of achievement, a believer should remain humble and grateful.

Ayah 1-3

Reminder of Humility After Success

The Surah emphasizes gratitude to Allah after experiencing victory. The Prophet Muhammad ﷺ was instructed to humble himself, even after such a monumental success. This shows that success and victory are a result of Allah's mercy, and the believer must continue to seek His forgiveness.

Ayah 1-3

Prophetic Mission's Completion

Surah An-Nasr marks the end of the Prophet's ﷺ struggles with his enemies and the completion of his mission. The conquest of Makkah was the pivotal turning point in the spread of Islam. The Surah foretells that with the coming of victory, the work of spreading the message of Islam is essentially fulfilled.

Ayah 1-3

Spiritual Guidance

Surah An-Nasr teaches that divine support and victory come through faith, patience, and reliance on Allah. The Surah encourages humility, gratitude, and repentance, even in times of success. It also serves as a reminder that Allah is the true source of all victories.

Lessons to Learn

Victory comes from Allah alone: acknowledge His help in all successes.

Gratitude after success: always thank and praise Allah after achieving goals.

Repentance after success: don't become complacent; seek Allah's forgiveness.

Action Steps

Praise Allah for every success: take moments of victory to thank Him.

Stay humble: remember that success is by Allah's will.

Reflect on divine help in your struggles: trust that Allah's victory is with those who remain patient and faithful.

Revealed in	Juz	Surah No.	No. of verses
Makkah	30	111	5

سُورَةُ المَسَدِ

SURAH AL-MASAD

(THE PALM FIBER)

مَآ أَغْنَىٰ عَنْهُ مَالُهُۥ وَمَا كَسَبَ ۝

"Neither his wealth nor 'worldly' gains will benefit him." (111:2)

Context

This Surah was revealed against Abu Lahab, one of the fiercest enemies of Islam and the uncle of Prophet Muhammad ﷺ. When the Prophet ﷺ invited people to Islam, Abu Lahab insulted him, saying: "May you perish! Is this why you gathered us?" In response, Allah revealed this Surah, foretelling Abu Lahab's doom due to his arrogance, opposition, and hatred towards the Prophet ﷺ and Islam.

Topics

- Condemnation of Abu Lahab
- Punishment for Arrogance
- Punishment for Those Who Harm the Messenger ﷺ
- Failure of Wealth and Power to Protect From Divine Justice

Theme

Surah Al-Masad is a divine condemnation of Abu Lahab and his wife, who were among the greatest enemies of Islam. It highlights the consequences of arrogance, hostility toward truth, and rejection of faith. The Surah serves as a warning that wealth and power cannot save anyone from Allah's punishment if they persist in their disbelief and oppression.

Virtues & Benefits

A powerful warning against opposing Allah and His Messenger ﷺ.
Encourages believers to trust in Allah's justice and remain steadfast against opposition.

Ayah 1 — The Curse Upon Abu Lahab

Allah declares Abu Lahab's destruction, emphasizing that both his actions (hands) and his own self are doomed. This verse highlights the certainty of divine punishment for those who oppose the truth and harm Allah's Messenger ﷺ. His hostility towards Islam ensured his eternal loss.

Ayah 2 — Wealth & Power Will Not Save Him

Despite being one of the wealthiest men in Makkah, Abu Lahab's riches and social status could not save him from Allah's decree. This verse proves that material possessions hold no value in the face of divine punishment if a person is corrupt and arrogant.

Ayah 3 — The Torment of Hellfire

Allah warns that Abu Lahab will suffer in Hellfire, referred to as a blazing flame (Lahab), ironically matching his name. This verse reaffirms that opposition to truth leads to eternal suffering and that even those with high worldly status will face divine justice.

Ayah 4 — The Role of His Wife in Evil

Abu Lahab's wife, Umm Jamil, was equally hostile toward Islam. She spread slander, abuse, and even placed thorns in the Prophet's ﷺ path. The phrase "carrier of firewood" symbolizes her fueling of hatred and hints at her punishment in Hell where she will carry firewood to intensify her own torment.

Ayah 5 — The Punishment of Abu Lahab's Wife

Umm Jamil, known for her arrogance and cruelty, will be humiliated in Hell with a rope of palm fiber tied around her neck. This verse symbolizes her disgrace and suffering, showing that those who harm Allah's Messenger will face severe consequences.

Ayah 1-5 — Summary of the Surah

This Surah serves as a warning against arrogance, hatred, and enmity towards Islam. Abu Lahab and his wife used their status and wealth to oppose the truth, yet they faced utter humiliation and destruction. This teaches that true success lies in faith, not in wealth or social power.

Lessons to Learn

Enemies of Islam will ultimately fail: Abu Lahab's wealth and status could not save him.

Wealth and power are worthless without faith: They do not grant safety from Allah's punishment.

Divine justice is inevitable: Allah's promise of punishment is always fulfilled.

Action Steps

Do not let wealth and power blind you from faith.

Trust in Allah's justice when facing opposition or hardship.

Be mindful of how you treat others, especially those who spread goodness.

Avoid arrogance and hostility toward truth.

سُورَةُ الإِخْلَاصِ

SURAH AL-IKHLAS

(THE SINCERITY)

Revealed in	Juz	Surah No.	No. of verses
Makkah	30	112	4

قُلْ هُوَ ٱللَّهُ أَحَدٌ ۝ ٱللَّهُ ٱلصَّمَدُ ۝ لَمْ يَلِدْ وَلَمْ يُولَدْ ۝ وَلَمْ يَكُن لَّهُۥ كُفُوًا أَحَدٌۢ ۝

"Say, 'O Prophet,' "He is Allah—One 'and Indivisible'; Allah—the Sustainer 'needed by all'. He has never had offspring, nor was He born. And there is none comparable to Him." (112:1-4)

Context

This Surah was revealed when the polytheists of Makkah asked Prophet Muhammad ﷺ about the nature of Allah, saying: "Describe your Lord to us." In response, Allah revealed Surah Al-Ikhlas, which defines His absolute oneness, uniqueness, and independence. It refutes all forms of polytheism and affirms Tawhid (Islamic monotheism) in its purest form.

Topics

- Oneness of Allah (Tawhid)
- Allah's Absolute Self-Sufficiency
- Refutation of All Forms of Polytheism
- Rejection of Any Likeness to Allah

Theme

Surah Al-Ikhlas is a powerful declaration of Tawhid, emphasizing Allah's absolute oneness and uniqueness. It rejects any notion of partners, offspring, or dependence in Allah's being. This Surah serves as the foundation of Islamic faith, encapsulating the essence of belief in one God who is eternal, self-sufficient, and beyond comparison.

Virtues & Benefits

Reciting it three times earns the reward of reciting the whole Qur'an.
It offers protection and spiritual purification when recited sincerely.

Ayah 1

The Oneness of Allah (Tawhid)

This verse establishes that Allah is uniquely One, without partners or equals. The word "Ahad" signifies an absolute, indivisible oneness, unlike anything in creation. This verse is a direct rejection of polytheism and affirms that Allah alone is the true God, deserving of worship.

Ayah 2

Allah, the Self-Sufficient Master

Allah is As-Samad, meaning completely self-sufficient, needing nothing while all creation depends on Him. He is the provider, sustainer, and ultimate source of security. This verse reassures believers that they can turn to Allah for all needs, as He is unaffected by time, weakness, or dependency.

Ayah 3

Allah Has No Offspring

This verse refutes the idea that Allah has children or was born from anyone. Many religions claim God has a son or is part of a lineage, but Islam firmly rejects this notion. Allah is eternal and uncreated, with no beginning or end, making Him beyond human attributes.

Ayah 4

Allah Is Beyond Comparison

This verse declares that nothing in existence is like Allah. No human, angel, deity, or concept can compare to His greatness. Unlike creation, He has no weaknesses or limitations. This verse seals the message of pure Tawhid, affirming Allah's absolute uniqueness.

Ayah 1-4

Surah's Power in Faith & Worship

Surah Al-Ikhlas is called "one-third of the Qur'an" due to its emphasis on Tawhid. The Prophet ﷺ stated that reciting it three times is equivalent to reciting the entire Qur'an. It is frequently used in prayers and daily supplications to reaffirm belief in Allah's absolute oneness.

Ayah 1-4

A Declaration of Sincerity & Pure Faith

The Surah's title, Al-Ikhlas (Sincerity), reflects that belief in Allah's oneness must be pure and free from any form of shirk (associating partners with Allah). Reciting it sincerely brings spiritual rewards, protection, and closeness to Allah. This Surah is a complete statement of faith and a shield against misguidance.

Lessons to Learn

Allah is One and Unique: No one shares in His power, attributes, or essence.

Allah has no children or parents: Unlike creation, He is eternal and beyond lineage.

No one compares to Allah: He is beyond any human imagination or resemblance.

Action Steps

Recite Surah Al-Ikhlas daily in prayers, morning/evening Adhkar, and before sleeping.

Use it for protection by reciting it regularly, as recommended by the Prophet ﷺ.

Reflect on its meaning to strengthen belief in Allah's absolute oneness.

Revealed in	Juz	Surah No.	No. of verses
Makkah	30	113	5

سُورَةُ الفَلَق

SURAH AL-FALAQ

(THE DAYBREAK)

قُلْ أَعُوذُ بِرَبِّ ٱلْفَلَقِ ۝ مِن شَرِّ مَا خَلَقَ ۝ وَمِن شَرِّ غَاسِقٍ إِذَا وَقَبَ ۝ وَمِن شَرِّ
ٱلنَّفَّٰثَٰتِ فِى ٱلْعُقَدِ ۝ وَمِن شَرِّ حَاسِدٍ إِذَا حَسَدَ ۝

"Say, 'O Prophet,' "I seek refuge in the Lord of the daybreak from the evil of whatever He has created, and from the evil of the night when it grows dark, and from the evil of those 'witches casting spells by' blowing onto knots, and from the evil of an envier when they envy." (113:1-5)

Context

Surah Al-Falaq was revealed to seek refuge in Allah from various forms of evil. It specifically addresses the dangers of black magic, envy, and the harmful effects of the unseen forces. The Surah was revealed during a time when the Prophet Muhammad ﷺ was facing various types of opposition, including magic and witchcraft.

Topics

- Seeking Refuge From the Harm of the Night and Darkness
- Protection From the Evil of Jealousy and Envy
- Trust in Allah's Power for Protection
- Protection from Witchcraft

Theme

The central theme of Surah Al-Falaq is seeking Allah's protection from external harm. The Surah asks Allah for refuge from the darkness of the night, the evil of jealousy, sorcery, and all harmful creatures or influences. It reminds believers to turn to Allah alone for protection from the unseen dangers of life.

Virtues & Benefits

Surah Al-Falaq, and Surah An-Nas, is often recited for protection from harmful forces and evil. Reciting the Surah regularly can bring peace of mind and protect from jealousy.

Ayah 1
Seeking Refuge in the Lord of Dawn

The Surah begins with a declaration of seeking protection in Allah, the Lord of Al-Falaq (Daybreak). The word Falaq symbolizes the break of dawn, representing Allah's power to remove darkness and bring forth light. Just as dawn dispels night, Allah alone can shield believers from all harm, both physical and spiritual. This verse emphasizes absolute trust in Allah as the ultimate protector.

Ayah 2
Protection from Evils of Creation

Allah's creation includes both goodness and potential harm. This verse reminds believers to seek refuge from the negative aspects of creation, such as diseases, harmful creatures, and malicious people. While Allah allows trials as tests, He alone can grant protection from them. The believer, therefore, acknowledges their vulnerability and turns to Allah for absolute safety from all forms of harm.

Ayah 3
Darkness and Unseen Dangers

Nighttime represents uncertainty, hidden threats, and fear. In ancient times, darkness concealed wild animals, criminals, and supernatural dangers. Today, it symbolizes anxiety, fear of the unknown, and unseen spiritual forces. This verse urges believers to turn to Allah during times of vulnerability, ensuring protection from both physical and unseen dangers that may lurk in the dark.

Ayah 4
Protection from Sorcery & Black Magic

This verse refers to black magic and sorcery, practiced by those who tie knots and blow spells upon them. Islam acknowledges the reality of magic but teaches that Allah's power surpasses all supernatural harm. Seeking refuge in Allah ensures protection from witchcraft, curses, and negative spiritual influences, reinforcing that faith in Allah is the strongest shield against all evil forces.

Ayah 5
Protection from Envy and Jealousy

Jealousy (hasad) is a destructive emotion that can lead to hatred, plotting, and even spiritual harm. The concept of the evil eye (ayn) is also linked to envy, where a person's intense jealousy can unknowingly harm others. This verse teaches believers to seek Allah's protection from envious individuals, ensuring that their blessings remain safeguarded from negative intentions.

Ayah 1-5
Summary of Surah Al-Falaq

Surah Al-Falaq emphasizes that Allah alone grants true protection from all forms of harm—whether from creation, darkness, magic, or envy. It serves as a daily reminder to trust in Allah's power rather than fearing external threats. By regularly reciting this Surah, believers affirm their reliance on divine security, seeking Allah's refuge in every aspect of life.

Lessons to Learn

The importance of seeking refuge in Allah from all forms of harm, particularly those from unseen forces such as jealousy & witchcraft,

It teaches the power of seeking Allah's protection and the significance of turning to Him for help in both seen and unseen trials.

The believer should turn to Allah and trust in His power to safeguard them from harm

Action Steps

Make a habit of reciting Surah Al-Falaq, especially before sleeping, to seek protection from harm during the night.

When facing jealousy, envy, or harm from others, recite this Surah as a shield to protect yourself spiritually.

Teach children and loved ones to recite this Surah for their protection and well-being.

Revealed in	Juz	Surah No.	No. of verses
Makkah	30	114	6

سُورَةُ النَّاسِ

SURAH AN-NAAS

(THE PEOPLE)

قُلْ أَعُوذُ بِرَبِّ ٱلنَّاسِ ۝ مَلِكِ ٱلنَّاسِ ۝ إِلَٰهِ ٱلنَّاسِ ۝ مِن شَرِّ ٱلْوَسْوَاسِ ٱلْخَنَّاسِ ۝
ٱلَّذِى يُوَسْوِسُ فِى صُدُورِ ٱلنَّاسِ ۝ مِنَ ٱلْجِنَّةِ وَٱلنَّاسِ ۝

"Say, 'O Prophet,' "I seek refuge in the Lord of humankind, the Master of humankind, the God of humankind, from the evil of the lurking whisperer— who whispers into the hearts of humankind— from among jinn and humankind." (114:1-6)

Context

Surah An-Nas was revealed to seek refuge in Allah from the harmful influence of evil beings, particularly from the harm caused by human whisperings, Shaytaan, and jealousy. It serves as a reminder that Allah alone has the power to protect one from all external and internal harms, especially from the influence of negative energies.

Topics

- Seeking Refuge From Evil Whispers
- Ongoing Need for Allah's Protection
- Allah as the Ultimate Protector
- Protection From Jealousy
- Seeking Divine Help to Maintain Spiritual Purity and Safety.

Theme

The central theme of Surah An-Nas is seeking Allah's protection from all forms of evil, particularly from the whisperings and temptations of Shaytaan, and harmful influences from human beings. The Surah emphasizes turning to Allah for refuge in times of distress and harm, seeking His aid for spiritual protection against all evil.

Virtues & Benefits

Surah An-Nas is a powerful invocation for protection against all forms of evil.
It is considered one of the last two protective Surah's (along with Surah Al-Falaq).

Ayah 1

Seeking Refuge in the Lord of People

The Surah begins by seeking refuge in Allah, who is the Lord of humankind. This verse acknowledges that Allah is the master of all people, and by seeking His refuge, the believer is asking for His protection from any harm caused by human or other malevolent forces.

Ayah 2

Seeking Protection from the Sovereign

This verse refers to Allah as the Sovereign of people. He alone has control over everything, including the hearts and minds of individuals. The believer calls upon Allah for protection from the evil whispers that may come from others, acknowledging His complete authority over all creation.

Ayah 3

Seeking Refuge in the God of People

The third verse emphasizes that Allah is the ultimate God of all people. By seeking refuge in Him, the believer is acknowledging Allah's exclusive right to guide, protect, and provide for His creation. It highlights Allah's role as the ultimate source of safety and security for humankind.

Ayah 4

Protection from Evil Whispers

The Surah continues by seeking protection from the evil whisperings of Satan, who attempts to lead humans astray. These whispers may come in the form of doubts, temptations, and negative thoughts. The believer seeks refuge in Allah from these internal threats that seek to disturb their peace of mind.

Ayah 5

Protection from the Evil of the Devil

This verse specifically mentions the evil of the devil (Shaytan), whose goal is to mislead people into sin and spiritual corruption. The believer asks Allah to protect them from this malevolent force, which is a constant source of temptation and harm.

Ayah 6

Protection from the Evil of Humans

The Surah concludes by seeking protection from the harm caused by the whisperings of people, especially those with ill intentions, jealousy, and hatred. It emphasizes that people can sometimes cause harm through their negative thoughts, words, or actions, and the believer seeks refuge from this harm as well.

Lessons to Learn

The importance of seeking Allah's protection from the harmful influences of the unseen world and the seen world (such as people with malicious intentions)

Only Allah has the ultimate power it highlights that only Allah has the ultimate power to provide protection from all harm.

It emphasizes the power of divine refuge and the necessity of turning to Allah for spiritual safety.

Action Steps

Recite Surah An-Nas regularly, especially before sleeping, to seek refuge from harm and negative energies.

Use the Surah as a tool for spiritual purification invoking Allah's protection from jealousy, ill intentions, and Satan's whispers.

In times of anxiety or distress recite this Surah to calm the mind and seek divine help in difficult situations.